"Are you riding an emotional roller coaster? One receives the beauty unfolding in the circle of life as Gail portrays her path to enlightenment. A story of the process of a daughter's love found through the poetry of her mother's fatal battle with cancer: a journey that takes one beyond the human dimension of understanding the process of death and re-birth. A 'must read' for a grieving family."

Christina Lorraine
Reiki Practitioner
Tustin, California

"The author takes you on a soul-searching journey through her life and her mother's, sending your emotions out of control... the sadness, the anger, the love. A heart-wrenching story to remind you to laugh and forgive in your own life."

Michele Dazey-Niston
Customer Service Supervisor at BREG, Inc.
Vista, California

"This very giving author shares her mother's dying gift of love which allows her to forgive, and thereby awaken the unconditional love between mother and daughter. Her words remind us that only through forgiveness, can we experience the love we all search for."

Nancy Rogala
Vista, California

I0807751

"I Am A Thousand Winds That Blow"

The Healing Power of a Remarkable Death

"I Am A Thousand Winds That Blow"

The Healing Power of a Remarkable Death

by

Gail Michael

BONNEVILLE BOOKS™
Springville, Utah

ISBN: 1-55517-611-9
e.3

Published by Bonneville Books
Imprint of Cedar Fort Inc.
www.cedarfort.com

Distributed by:

Typeset by Kristin Nelson
Cover design by Adam Ford
Cover design © 2002 by Lyle Mortimer

Printed in the United States of America
10 9 8 7 6 5 4 3 2 1

Printed on acid-free paper

Library of Congress Cataloging-in-Publication Data

Michael, Gail, 1954-
I am a thousand winds that blow : the healing power of a remarkable death / by Gail Michael.
p. cm.
ISBN 1-55517-611-9 (pbk. : alk. paper)
1. Grief. 2. Bereavement--Psychological aspects. 3. Mothers--Death--Psychological aspects. 4. Mothers and daughters. I. Title: Healing power of a remarkable death. II. Title.
BF575.G7 .M52 2002
155.9'37--dc21

2002003217

Dedication

With my deepest and most profound love,
I dedicate this book to my mother,
Alyce Jane Ouelette Henricks

Acknowledgments

My heartfelt thanks to all of may family and friends who have supported me and stood by me throughout my life, with no judgment, no matter what path I was on, or what direction I was headed.

I thank my guides, teachers and angels, both carnate and incarnate, and my beloved Guru Isa Mafu.

I also thank Cedar Fort, Inc., for believing in me enough to make my dream come true of sharing my mother's story with the world.

TABLE OF CONTENTS

Introduction

Have you recently lost a loved one or are you facing this challenge now? If so, this book is for you. It is the story of my mother, our relationship and her long battle with lung cancer. It offers hope and comfort to those of you who are afraid and for those that are in the process of passing into their new life, their rebirth.

For the last year of her life, my mother made peace with herself and her loved ones and healed her fractured family. We, too, as her children, went through the same process. At times it was sad for us, but never for her. There was no fear, only laughter.

Dying from this earth plane and going on to the next, should not be a time filled with fear, darkness sadness or depression. It should be a time of great love and support, a time of laughter and shared memories. As my mother lived through her final days on earth, she reviewed her life as a human and also was able to share with us what was happening on the other side. They threw a party for her, and all of her loved ones were there.

I hope as you read this, it offers you some insight of what you can expect before, during and after the "rebirth." And I hope that it gives you strength and peace of mind to know that your loved ones are being delivered into the arms of those who love them.

—Gail Michael

"My life has woven a story–
one to speak of, and–
to learn from.
It has had its hills and valleys,
but mostly, it
brought me back to the blue seas.
I never forgot what I was there to do, and
I never forgot "HE"
who stood beside me–
always.

It was a wondrous journey, and
a wondrous life,
full of passion and pain–
sunshine and rain.
And my people came into my life,
one by one–
to remind me of their love for me, and
of mine for them.
And to show me how beauteous it was–

to be loved by mankind–
as a human.

As I reached the end of my journey,
it did not matter that I–
no longer spoke their names.
It only mattered–
that I
held them in my heart,
to remain with me–
forever."

Chapter 1

The Voice

"***You need to forgive her. She is dying, you know.***" The voice was loud and clear. I was in my car driving back from the gardens overlooking the ocean. This was my sacred place and also the one I had shared with the spirit of my mother whenever I was troubled, hurt, angry or sad; I'd come here to the Self-Realization Fellowship gardens (SRF). It was a place free for anyone to enjoy, even if you were not a devotee. The beach down below, Swami's Beach, was a special place where I could be with her.

I was drawn to come here so strongly on this day. I thought about Mom because I hadn't spoken to her in nine months. We had shared some hurtful moments and were unable to rise above them. I had come here in January and mentally "tossed her" (or a representation of her), into the sea. I had cried uncontrollably. I thought about her as I meditated and sat quietly. I was at peace in that moment as I had always been when I sat to meditate, for it gave me that inner strength I so needed to rely on every day.

As I headed north on the I-5 freeway, the voice spoke to me, "*You need to forgive her. She is dying, you know.*" I thought about that for a moment, and then, without hesitation, trusting Spirit, I knew I had to reconnect with her. Her birthday was coming up in a few weeks, so I decided to write to her and send her a birthday card. Perhaps hat would open the door.

Decent conversations had been difficult between us most of our lives. It seemed Mom was always hard on me, angry with me, and often disappointed in me. I could never seem to live up to her expectations. And I was never truly clear on what those expectations were. Her shadow followed me from the east coast to the west coast and still "shadowed" me after I left home twenty-one years earlier.

This was our relationship, as I knew it.

> And she said, "*Mommy, what do you think our purpose is while we are here?*"
>
> *"What do you think it is, little one?"*
>
> *"Well, I think we are supposed to learn something, and take it to the next place so we can use it there. But I don't know what it is yet."*

My mother was born in the small city of Taunton, Massachusetts on the memorable date of September 11th, 1935. She had one sibling, an older sister Jeannette. I never knew much about her life. Now I realize how sad it is that I never sat with her and asked her to share her childhood memories with me. I question my friends and people I meet on the streets but regret I did not take the time to do that with my mother. The only memories she passed on to me were of an unhappy childhood where she felt she was an unwanted child. Her sister was favored and her mother was always angry with her. She loved her dad to pieces. I do remember that after my grandmother passed away my mom spent quite a bit of time with her dad.

During my mother's difficult teenage years, she fell in love with my father who was 6 ft. 7 inches." She was a mere 5 ft. He was a very handsome man who looked like Elvis. Mom was pretty, too. Dad would get drunk, sit up on the parking meters in town and serenade her with his trumpet. She couldn't resist her attraction to the "bad boy," and became pregnant at seventeen with my sister, Carol. As I remember the story, she climbed out of the second story window of the house to elope. Her dreams were to live "*happily ever after*." Unfortunately, my father, an alcoholic, wasn't a very pleasant person to be around when he was drunk. After they married, life was very difficult for Mom. Dad wouldn't come home on payday. Instead, he would stay out drinking and gambling all night, and when he did come home, he would beat my mother. When she was nine months pregnant with my younger sister, he pushed her down the stairs.

She would not go home to her mother's house and she would never ask for help. How could she? She felt she was not wanted or loved by her mother, so she suffered in silence, like many women of her generation. By the time she was twenty-six, she had four children: Carol was eight, I was six, my brother was four, and she had a new baby. Her husband wasn't coming home with a paycheck and there was no money for food. Every one of us, including her, were crying and starving, suffering inside the prison she called home. She was barely an adult with adult responsibilities and burdens.

I think back upon my childhood with all of its lost memories and realize that Mom was probably so depressed she could barely function. Finally she decided to leave him. She moved back into the house with no love–her parents' house. My memories were of my aunt and three of us kids in one bedroom, my mother, grandmother and baby sister in my grandmother's room and my grandfather in his own room. (My mother told me that after she was born, her parents stopped sleeping together. I think she always thought it was her fault).

This was Mom's life, as she knew it to be.

Oh, my beloved.
Where are you?
Where did you go?
All I can see is the darkness
that has trapped me—
in my cell of a room.

For three years, Mother and her four children lived with my grandparents. Life there was never happy or pleasant . . . or was that just from my perspective? We didn't have any running water in the bathroom (except for the toilet), so we bathed in the big kitchen sink where we washed dishes. Grammy also washed all our laundry in that sink, wringing each piece out by hand. Mom worked as a waitress at a pizza parlor for a few dollars an hour, relying on her tips. I remember her working long and hard and not wanting to stand on her feet when she got home. We saw my father a few times after she left him, but the visits stopped quickly.

I do have memories of my grandfather's heavy drinking and my grandmother's anger and constant yelling. She was such an unhappy woman that I don't ever remember a smile on her face. Those were very depressing years–for us as children as well as for my mother. After what seemed like a lifetime in this house, we moved to our own place in the projects. We children were so happy there that my mom was relieved. She finally had her own space and her own room and was living her life as an adult. With assistance from Aid for Dependent Children, (ADC) and her waitressing job, we were able to scrape by.

Mom's hours were long and hard and we talked to her more on the telephone than in person. She worked five to six days a week, ten hours a day. She was always so tired, sleeping constantly when she came home. I think her body needed all that rest, while her mind wanted to escape. I remember lots of yelling when we were loud or out of control because we were fighting with each other. At those times, she would retreat into her room and shut the door, sometimes not coming out for twenty-four hours at a time. We were on pins and needles waiting for her to accept our apologies, but to no avail. It never even occurred to me as a child to knock on the door and ask her if I could come in. If I had hugged her in those times or said, "I love you", maybe things would have been different. None of us, including Mom, would have known to do that. No example had ever been set.

When she was locked in her room trying to deal with these times, I now realize she was dealing with depression. I am surprised that she made it through, having no help and no one to rely on except her four children, and we were too young to know how to support her emotionally.

Alas,
I have found you inside these walls
I have built around myself.

Who would have thought
you would be here –
to keep me company?

While we lived in the projects, Mom's mother died. I never knew how she died. I only remember being told when I was young that it was possibly food poisoning. I remember hearing that an autopsy was never done. There was a lot left unsaid in our lives because we just didn't talk about things. And we didn't know to ask. Silence seemed to be the way of those times, or the way of my family.

My mom and grandmother had stopped speaking to each other after we moved out. I never knew why. Was it because she moved out and my grandmother didn't think she was ready? I don't even know if Mom was sad when her mother passed away, or hurt by the finality of the separation. We saw more of my grandfather after that; he seemed happier than I remembered. He smiled and laughed a lot and I saw my mother smile when he was there. He spent holiday dinners with us and I even have a memory of Grandpa sitting next to our silver Christmas tree. That moment stands out in my mind for some reason, probably because of the big smile on his face.

Tragically, Grandpa died in a fire in his apartment building. He was a heavy drinker who loved his vodka and had many lost days and nights. He fell asleep with a lit cigarette and burned down the building. Mom took it hard. She felt that the one true person she had in her life who loved her was now gone.

Her depression returned after that. She spent nearly all of her time at work, and when she was home, she spent more and more time asleep in her room–even during the day. She did make sure we had a vacation, however–every year or two to a cabin on a lake. Usually it was with either friends of the family or another single mom she worked with.

Mom never had a social life. She never went out with the girls or on dates. She did see one man during my teenage years, but it was short-lived probably because he was extremely abusive. I remember lying in my bed at night listening to them and actually hearing her whimper pitifully as he hit her. I was very happy when he stopped coming around. She dated one man when I was in my twenties and one when I was in my thirties. All of them treated her poorly. There was always some type of abuse involved, or they were alcoholics. All she knew with men was deception. Poor mom.

She continued to work hard, always waitressing. Everyone in town knew her and loved her. She was known for her great sense of humor and her love and loyalty as a friend, things I only learned upon her death. Financially, she struggled, but she never hung her head. She always kept it raised high with dignity and honor. I remember that visitors from ADC actually came in and made us turn on the television to make sure it wasn't "too ritzy" for us. They would go through our rooms to take a look, and every time mom got a small raise, they would reduce her aid check. She never had a car all the while we were growing up.

I remember her sitting down at the table every night counting her tips. She piled them separately: dimes, nickels, and quarters. Each pile she made would be earmarked for a new table or something unaffordable that we needed. She was tenacious, and she knew exactly what we needed, never giving up until we had enough to buy it. And she laughed about it, too. She could make money stretch and knew how to budget like no one I have ever met in my life. Unfortunately, I didn't inherit this trait.

This endless poverty began to wear on me. As I grew into my early teens, I became rebellious. I felt abandoned by both of my parents, and resented having to shoulder the responsibilities of caring for my siblings while mom worked "round the clock." Because my older sister Carol was mentally and emotionally handicapped, the burden seemed even more unfair. Although she had never been diagnosed as being mentally handicapped, the public school system had placed her in a special needs class, which consisted of children with Down syndrome and with other mental and physical disabilities. Throughout her childhood, my sister would mimic all her classmates' tendencies. She would pick up their speech patterns and behavioral styles. She was a sweet, loving child, but to this day she acts emotionally and mentally as a ten-year-old would.

My brother was the quiet one. He was three years younger than me and we were very close throughout our childhood. You never knew what was going on inside his head, but when he spoke, it was usually profound. He was brilliant inside himself and I don't think he ever realized how brilliant he was and still is. I also remember him as a great writer and poet.

Lisa, my baby sister, was seven years younger than me, and was least affected by our childhood. She was a baby when we left my father so she had no memories of those times. She was Mom's special sweet spot. Every day, she would say something cute like, *"Mommy, what would happen to me if I fell inside my milk?"* She called turkey dressing "*tressy.*" She was so cute with this sweet smile she always had for Mom. She made Mom laugh when I thought there was no hope in my confused teenage mind.

Mom and I grew further and further apart. It was heart-breaking to experience. We loved each other but we could not get past ourselves to tell the other how we felt. After our angry fights, we would write what I called "tear-your-heart-out-letters" to each other and leave them on the kitchen table. As I became more rebellious, my mother retreated further into her room, her sleep and her depression.

And the wings of the falcon
Came down and covered the earth.
And the Lord spoke,

"Unto this day,
I will give you anything you wish for–
For you have been the power
And the love within me,
And you have shown me that love."

"Do not be afraid–
for you may have anything,
and all that you need–
to survive this journey.

I love you.

Chapter 2

The Veil

Those painful childhood years set the tone for the type of relationship I would have with Mom throughout our lives until her final year. I always felt that we never understood each other and I didn't have a clue as to what she was going through all those years. I always felt that she expected too much from me, that whatever I did wasn't good enough. I could never live up to her expectations. She was always angry with me, reprimanding me or yelling at me; or she was taking to her bed when she was angry, giving me the silent treatment. I was so confused.

I had my own problems too. I did not fare well during my childhood. either emotionally or physically. I wondered: How could four children in the same family, all have such different views of their childhoods and end up so different from each other? I wondered if it was dependent upon our emotional strengths and weaknesses at the time? Do our experiences with our friends and other family members influence how we perceive our lives? All I know is that while I struggled to stay sane and healthy in my life, our relationship broke apart into fragments. What made this happen? The result of my painful childhood was almost total memory loss, physical illness, and depression with suicidal tendencies and unhealthy relationships with men. I didn't have very strong, long-lasting friendships, either. It would take a few years of therapy and getting hit in the head with a few bricks before I would open up and trust anyone enough to learn what I needed to learn from them. My lessons were hard and seemed to take forever. Therefore, I always seemed to be in a bad relationship that I should have gotten out of years before. I attracted the wrong types of men, too. I didn't know how to set boundaries or pay attention to the red flags. I wanted all of them to like me and take care of me. I felt I wasn't worthy of being loved, so I would do anything to make them see that I was a great catch. It was all so sick and sordid. I had no idea. I was still a little girl inside.

I was never really successful in my career, either. I always seemed to have an angel sitting on my shoulder or guiding me, though. I would always end up with a good job. The hard part for me was finding happiness and fulfillment in one specific career or job and sticking around long enough to succeed even further. I couldn't commit in any aspect of my life. It amazes me that I fell in love and stayed married long enough to have my wonderful son.

When my life began,
you were holding my hand.
Then,
you let go.

In my childhood,
I would–
glimpse you in the nigh–
and feel your fingertips upon my heart.

As I grew older,
you never left my side, and
spoke my name, so that I
would always remember you.

Eventually, we all grew up. At twenty-one, I moved out, and mistook my "freedom" for "license" to destroy myself. Finally, at twenty-five, after four years of experimenting with drugs and alcohol, one of my relationships took me to California. It just happened. It seemed to be an angel from heaven that got me there. It doesn't matter what the reason was or that the relationship didn't last. It lifted me up and moved me far away from the self-destruction, the depression, the responsibility of caring for my mother emotionally . . . not that she had ever asked me to care for her. I had just always assumed that it was my responsibility to care for her needs.

She didn't speak to me for that first year. I moved the first week in December and that Christmas she wouldn't take my telephone calls. She was punishing me for leaving her, abandoning her, like everyone else in her life had. I was re-living all those years before when she would go into her room and lock me out, using the silent punishment. That is what I thought she was doing. For twelve months she wouldn't take my calls. I don't even know if she read my cards or letters. There was never a response. I was devastated. I had lost my mother. The pain was great. I carried it around inside of myself, turning the emotional pain into endometriosis, stomach ulcers, ulcerative colitis, Epstein-Barr and just general pain that usually caused me to pass out. I was twenty-five and so sick most of the time that I fainted constantly and had to be driven home from work or from dinner by my boyfriend. I was some piece of work!

I didn't really want to live and was punishing myself for all the guilt I held for abandoning my mother, my mentally handicapped older sister and my other two siblings. I bolted. I ran away from it all. I was too scared to stay and face the music of my life–of their lives. If things got too ugly or too abusive in my relationships or even friendships, I would stay in it and hang on for years sometimes, until I was physically ill and hardly had the strength to leave it. Or I would run away from it altogether. I felt trapped in any kind of a relationship–like a bird in a locked cage. I think that's why I always got so ill. I was dying on the inside.

Every day I would drive to my job and say to myself, *"I can do this. I am successful. I am happy. I am intelligent and beautiful. I love my life."* I would use this mantra to convince myself that I was worthy. It must have looked good on the outside, because it helped me move up in my career. It was divine guidance. My success was not of my own doing. I could not face the inside of my head. (Someone sweet once told me, "Don't go inside your head alone. It's a dangerous neighborhood. Take a friend with you.") On the inside, I was still the little girl that couldn't do anything right because I had failed my mother. She was unhappy with me and I loved her so much. I just wanted to be loved by her in return.

Instead of expressing my anger with her, I turned it inward. I was so confused and didn't understand anything. I was a lost soul with no direction, no family and worst of all, no mother. She only existed on the telephone and I grieved for the next twenty-one years that I no longer had a mother.

"A Mother–
always there.
Someone close–
So close, you were 'one'
at one time,
and then separated.

But you didn't know how to stop
the separation,
so you moved on–
far away.

And it took you forever–
to find your way back home—
to Mother–
the womb–
Like a rose,
with outstretched arms for you.

She was always waiting,
content with being who she was–
While you struggled to find
your identity.
'Which mask am I,' you asked?
It took forever–
or so it seemed,
before you realized–
that you were none of them.

There was no mask that fit.
So you removed them all,
and returned–
to the womb–
the home of your mother.
She wrapped you up–
inside her arms so sweet,
before her passing,
to show you,
she had always been there–
for You."

For twelve months, I called regularly–but she never would talk with me. Finally, at the end of that year, she picked up the phone and talked to me like we had never stopped talking to each other. It was the strangest thing, and we never discussed it. Out of nowhere, my mom was back.

Over the next twenty years as I lived my life on the West Coast, I married and had a child, divorced and remarried. Mom and I continued to talk on the telephone every few weeks or sometimes only once a month. I sent pictures and sometimes videos of my family, but only made the trip back every few years. I always had a good excuse not to go. Now, as I look back, I think it was sheer terror. It was very difficult for me to go back. I couldn't trust that it would be safe for me and I couldn't trust that I would know how to take care of myself in that environment. How silly, but it was my reality in that crazy neighborhood inside my head. I loved my mother, but had never felt loved by her.

Inside my head, I was never good enough to be successful in any endeavor in my life. I had married a wonderful husband and father to my son and had a wonderful stepson. I had good solid jobs that were lucrative and I had been very well taken care of when I married. But I never felt successful in anything. After my divorce, I struggled with unhealthy relationships. I didn't know how to set boundaries, and always seemed to set myself up in relationships where I couldn't live up to someone else's expectations. I also had control issues; therefore, I attracted men that would try to show me those issues by trying to control me. I was obsessed with order and cleanliness. It was the opposite end of the spectrum from my childhood. I actually felt I couldn't breathe when I was somewhere unclean or cluttered.

I firmly believe that when we are born into this world, we get to choose our parents, our birth dates, our families, the people we will meet on our journey called life, our circumstances, physical ailments, and so forth. We set ourselves up with different pathways so we can make choices. We create or lay these plans before we arrive at birth. We make our life plan, or blueprint. And the reason we make these choices is to experience certain emotions that will help our souls expand. When we expand and learn our lessons, then we can move on and pass over to our next destination.

My mother was my greatest teacher in this lifetime. And I thank her for the lessons she taught me. It took me forty-five years to understand and accept that she taught me these things because she loved me and wanted to make me a stronger, gentler, more compassionate human being. I believe I had chosen her to be my teacher. All of these conditions of both my parents and my childhood led me to this point in my life, this conscious, spiritual dance that I do every day. It took me years of therapy to understand my anger with God and to learn to forgive. My spiritual path taught me to learn how to love myself so that others would see my light shining from my inside out and know that I loved myself; therefore, I was lovable.

I began to forgive myself and to love myself. In the learning to love myself, I learned how to take care of "me" and how to draw the line and set boundaries in taking care of others. I was grieving again. I was saying good-bye to the old patterns, the old relationships and the old me. In all of this, my relationship with my mother was growing. I was learning things about her that I wasn't open to knowing before. There were things about her personality, her little quirks, her pet peeves, things she loved and hated. It was finally nice to know those things about her. We had a "nice" relationship. It was still mostly at a distance, but I did go home whenever I could now.

Until the last year of her life. . .

It happened one night. . .
My heart opened up, and
my soul burst forth–
with such enthusiasm!

I knew, I had to
follow,
or be lost–
forever!

Chapter 3

Acceptance, Allowance, Release

At age forty, three years after my divorce, I moved from California to Colorado to remarry once again, but it had failed. I was divorced within the year. For the next three years, I struggled in every aspect of my life. For every poor choice I made, I had to live with the consequences. Finally, in the fourth year, I was able to move back to my beloved western coastline in southern California. This was the true home I had set up for my son and myself–his birthplace. In the same way I lived my life, I made my move away from Colorado back to California—flying by the seat of my pants . With no commitments, I just followed my wild heart.

In California I had no job and nowhere to live. My son's father, my first husband was an angel and a gentleman. He took both my son and me in and we lived there for the next seven months while I continued to try to "find myself." I was in search of a new career. You see, if I stayed too long in one place or one job, I would be "committed" and then I would be that bird in the cage. I would die. Being committed to anything or anyone for any length of time would break me down. I had the overwhelming feeling that I was suffocating, dying. It's funny that the only commitment I have ever been able to make in my life was to my son. He was a gift from God. I never felt I was that "bird in the cage" with him. He lifted me up and inspired me. He was my gift from heaven. After my divorces and in my darkest hours, he was the reason I awoke each morning and got out of bed, the reason I was still alive. I didn't even think twice about my commitment to him. Then why couldn't I feel that for anything else or anyone else in life?

That Christmas morning, two months after my return to the west, with no home of my own and just barely a new job, I called my mother to wish her a happy Christmas. But she wouldn't take my call. I felt the same as I did twenty years ago, when she was angry with me. I felt I had failed again. I had failed enough. I didn't need to feel her disappointment, too. She wouldn't even speak with her grandson, my son. I unleashed all the anger I felt toward myself for failing and putting myself in this unstable place. I unleashed it on her. I cried all that day and often through the next few weeks. I was so sad.

I went to my gardens on the cliffside overlooking the beautiful Pacific and cried for hours. And then, symbolically, I threw her into the water. I told her I loved her, but I needed to let her go, so I could find happiness and accept myself without her looking over my shoulder to judge me. I said good-bye. That day in January of 1999 was one of the saddest days of my life.

I felt relieved. But I also felt empty. I felt like an orphan. I had not known my father for thirty-six years. Now I had said good-bye to my mother. It was a very difficult time. Somehow, I changed my focus on what I wanted in my life and I worked very hard toward that goal. I had to be successful. I couldn't live like this anymore. Over the next few months, I made it happen. I wanted my own home for my son and I and I wanted to make enough money so that we could live comfortably. I wanted to manage people and help them grow. I put a plan together and manifested all these things within five months. I was back on my feet, working hard and living in a place that I loved. I was living in the land of golden opportunities where the sun met the sea and dreams came true. I worked very hard and loved every day and every night that I shared with my son.

During that time, I meditated and prayed a lot. I was always one who asked for strength and guidance and the wisdom to see what I needed to learn. During my childhood I would say my prayers every night and ask God for the strength to go through another day and for time to move swiftly so that I would survive. I was afraid to ask for anything other than that for myself, because I thought that it was bad to do so.

Over the past ten years, I have learned to pray for guidance, assistance and the wisdom to understand. I looked within and sat with myself, welcoming who I was. At first, it was hard to be alone with myself. I wasn't afraid of anyone else out there that might hurt me; I was afraid of being alone with me! I would sometimes have anxiety attacks when I was alone with no plans, no friends and nothing to do. I think my greatest fear was that if I was by myself for too long, I would get to know *me* and see what kind of a person I really was and that I would be disappointed in what I saw.

So I prayed and prayed for self-love and acceptance. I went to the sea and sat with myself. It's funny how when life is trying to show you something, everything falls into place–or throws challenges at you that force you to learn. I found myself without many friends at that time in my life, so I was forced to be alone. Often I sat by the sea. It soothed my soul. I would often be so deeply depressed that I would frighten myself. I would never kill myself, but if I got really sick or run over by a car, I thought I wouldn't fight to stay alive. But the sound of the waves would quiet my mind and I found strength in that. When I meditated and prayed, I was in my heart, so my ego was asleep (or sitting quietly on the bank by the river).

I had such high expectations for myself, I was unforgiving

of my mistakes. When I did make mistakes, it would send me into a deep depression and a half pint of Haagen Dazs butter pecan ice cream. I binged when I was depressed. I didn't know how else to nurture myself. But I was finally conscious of what I was doing and I was learning how to nurture myself instead by buying flowers, or taking a bath with oils and candles, or sitting on the beach. Over those ten years, I finally got to meet Gail, allow her to be who she was and what she was, and to accept her. I was working hard on self-love.

In the first nine months of 1999, I started to realize I had shut myself off from not only my mother, but my friends, also. I had stepped back from all the people I loved and who loved me. In doing this, I felt I was in control of my life. If I were in control, no one would be able to hurt me. And there was no chaos in my life, only order. I was content for now, and finally loved being alive.

I went off to war
To slay all the demons and dragons
For you–
Until you told me that
They did not really exist.

As I sat in my car that January day in 2000 when I heard the voice, I thought about Mom and how much I loved her. Somewhere in the past nine months, I had finally come to realize that she had suffered a particularly difficult life. I felt sorry for her. I asked myself how she could love me the way I expected her to if she had never been loved in that way herself. I thought about her struggles, my childhood, how hard she had worked all her life, how she had cried out for love and respect, but had never received them from the men in her life or even her own mother. I thought how she had aged, not feeling well most of the time. She was always tired. I thought how she had slept on her days off because she was so exhausted. Even after she retired, she had to continue to work, because she couldn't live on the few hundred dollars per month she was given to live on.

I thought about my brother, who lived eight hours away by car with his family, who was as emotionally distant from Mom as I was with her. I thought about my distance and had regrets. I thought about my older sister who was mentally handicapped and how she disappeared when faced with any type of trauma or any confrontation at all. I thought of our fractured family in which most of us stopped speaking to one another when times got tough–or in emotional flare-ups. I understand now that when we did this, it was because one of us was hurt so badly that we couldn't see beyond our pain or anger. But I finally saw it all and thought how sad a life this was. After thinking about it for days, I sat down and wrote Mom a letter.

I wrote that it had been a very long time since we had spoken and that life was too short to hold any grudges. I told her finally about all the struggles with my life and how I had always felt that I could never live up to her expectations of me. Whether it was all fabricated in my mind or whether it was actually a reality, that was how I felt and it had to come from somewhere. I told her that I had allowed the tragedy of the family to effect me, but I wasn't going to allow it to happen to my son.

I also told her about the past nine months and what I had accomplished in my life. I sent pictures of her grandson and told her that I loved her. I said I would like to come home and visit when I could pull it all together. It was a very long letter. I wished her a happy birthday and sent it off with a birthday card. Everything I said was true and it felt good to finally put it on paper.

In speaking with my sister a few weeks later, I told her I had sent the letter. I didn't tell her about the voice and what was spoken. She said Mom had gotten the letter and was very happy that I wrote. She also said Mom would be sending me a birthday card. September was a big birthday month in our family because my mother's, my sister's and my birthdays were three weeks apart, and her sister's and her mother's were also within those same weeks.

The birthday card never came. What I got instead was the dreaded phone call from the baby of the family, Lisa. "Gail, I've got bad news. Mom has lung cancer and it has already metastasized into the liver and the brain." We spoke for quite a while, but I don't remember much of the conversation. I was stunned, but remembered the words that Spirit had spoken to me. As soon as we hung up, I called Mom. *"Mom, it's me, Gail. I heard you were sick. What's going on?"* She said, *"Oh, hello, Gail,"* and then she told me what the doctors had said. She then said, *"I don't want you worrying about me. I'll be fine. There's some pain, in my chest and I can't breathe, but they're giving me medicine for that. I'm just so tired all the time. I don't have the energy to get myself out of bed. That's depressing."*

We talked for about an hour but never touched on why we had stopped speaking. This was an old pattern of ours and of our family. We swept difficulties under the carpet in the hopes that they would go away. That was okay this time because the most important issue was Mom's health. Her spirits were up but I'm sure it was because I had written and called. I had seen how tied up in knots, how hurt and how depressed she had been in the past when my brother had not spoken to her for a while. She was relieved. How funny that so many mothers and daughters are so close, yet don't understand each other. We put so much energy into understanding our partners, our mates and our children, but we hold grudges with our mothers, sometimes until it's too late.

She was also relieved because her illness finally had a name. Now, the healing could begin, or so she thought. I told her in our conversation that I would be coming home for a visit soon and her first response, as always, was, *"Gail, don't waste your money. Spend it on something else. I will be fine. Stop worrying about me. Mom, I'm coming home anyway, so be quiet," I said.* The tone of this conversation was so different from any we ever had. There was no mask or ego between us now. There were more important issues to be discussed. There wasn't any time for the other stuff. We both talked for the first time without carrying around all that old hurt and anger. We were suddenly free from that. Reality had shocked us both into fear.

Over the next few months and the holidays, we spoke every few days and she updated me regularly on her progress. She went in for chemotherapy for weeks at a time and then she would stop, only to start another cycle. I prayed and meditated for guidance and understanding, and that I could give more love and compassion to her. I also prayed that she would make peace in her life so that she could pass over quickly and without pain. It wasn't that I wanted her to go quickly out of selfishness, but I had seen what cancer does to some and didn't want her to suffer. I also had confidence and peace because I knew what was on the other side.

During my life I had studied a lot on life after death. I had meditated on the subject, contemplated, and had visions of what was there. As a child, I would have dreams that I was there with the angels and with mother Mary, sitting on the clouds. I would fly and fly through the heavens, trying to escape those who were trying to take me back to earth, only to awaken in my bed. I would be feverish and ill and not want to wake up in my body. Mary would coax me into going back home. She told me she would always protect me and send the angels to watch over me. I had that same dream at least thirty times. I was angry that I had to stay on earth in a world where I felt I had been abandoned, without love. I wanted to go to the heavens where I could play and dance and fly and be surrounded with love. My only escape from this world that I dreaded was talking to "those from the other place," the safe and happy place I had come from in the beginning.

An angel awakened me this morning.
She held her fingertips to her lips, and whispered,
"Sshhh,"
and told me to come with her,
that she would show me
the way to heaven.

I slowly stepped from my bed and
followed–
out into the early morning air–
into the meadow–
into the sunrise.
I rose to the heavens, and
saw the stars that were there,
waiting for me.

Each one,
was an angel of light–
Each one–
shining love for those of us below.
With all their light,
we will find the way.

I was guided through breath-work,
and sound.
I was shown the inner secrets
to the universe, and was filled
with divine love.

And in that magnificent light,
I was brought home—
once again to awaken–
in my own world, and
to bring back what I had learned–
to the peoples of this earth.

Chapter 4

Love and Compassion

A great spiritual teacher I have studied with over the years, Ammagi from the "Foundation for Meditative Studies" in Oregon, had once shared with me her feelings on death and dying.

I share her views that we are born as humans to gain the power of compassion and perfect the ability to give love to all living things and to receive love. The human body is a shell, like that of a baby bird, protecting the spirit to be born until it is ready at death to live in the spirit environment. Your spirit is captured in the human egg, until in death, you achieve consciousness, awakening compassion. The meaning of death is to be born spiritually. So, in effect, it is a birth. To be born human is our human birth and to die is our spirit birth. Heaven is about happiness and joy, compassion and peace. The reason we don't remember the other side is because it is so beautiful and so filled with happiness, love, peace and beauty, that we wouldn't stay here. We would shed our bodies in death and leave immediately! I felt this was all true because of those repeated dreams I had so many times as a child. So I wanted my mother to pass quickly. I felt she deserved this wondrous birth after living in her life here.

Over the next few months, mom would convey to me all the physical symptoms she was going through. Chemo was hard on her, very hard, but she still did better with it then most. She lost her hair almost immediately, but she still had her appetite. On the sixth or seventh day after her chemo, she would be so sick that she was exhausted with no energy at all; she stayed inside her trailer alone and usually didn't see anyone. She was following doctor's orders, for on those days, her immune system was barely functioning.

She started to lose her vision in one eye and this frightened her. It started to close from the cancer. If she lost her vision, she would no longer be in control or independent. The eye was bandaged and she continued with the chemo. Over the next month, she became agitated with the bandage on her eye. She hated it because it was so bothersome and caused her to lose her equilibrium. Lisa said, *"Mom, take it off tonight when you go to bed. Give it a rest. It's staying closed on its own anyway."* So she did.

When she awoke the next morning, she was able to control the muscle so the eye opened and closed. She sat in her chair and although the vision was blurred, she was eventually able to see. It was a miracle to her. Her mood became upbeat and I think she thought she was being cured. Even though they told us in the beginning that she had small-cell cancer, which was fast-growing and incurable, even with the chemo, there was always hope of a miracle. There always is in life.

It was difficult for me to be so far away. I wanted to ask her oncologist so many questions. Though I had spoken to her in the beginning, I had not asked her about the eye. I assumed that tumors had been growing or pressing on the optic nerve or some nerve that affected the eye, and the chemo had now shrunk it, causing her vision to return. She returned to her daily crossword puzzles with ease. In one phone conversation she said, *"Gail, I love doing the puzzles. I think they keep my brain sharp. I don't know what I would have done if I could no longer do them."* I started to clip them from the California newspapers and collect them for her. It was like a project for me. In some small way, I felt I was helping her, giving her something she loved. Every week, I'd mail them out and she'd have tons more for the next week. I'd also send her newspaper clippings, cards and photographs. I'd send her letters sometimes, telling her all the things I never told her before. I told her I was proud of her and how she lived her life and that she had taught me so much, explaining each thing I learned. I told her I was proud to be her daughter and that she had been a good mom, that with what she was handed in life she had done the best she could. I told her that I knew she felt responsible for all the unhappiness or misfortune in her children's lives, but none of it was her fault.

I told her that I believed we came into this life with a blueprint that we had laid out before we were born, defining what we wanted for an outcome. We chose our parents, and together (future parent and child), we all chose the situations and defined all the circumstances that would mold our character. We chose our birth-dates, those people that would come into our lives, and we set many paths so that we had numerous choices. It was our own individual divine plan. In essence, we knew where our lives would take us before we came here. I believe we also chose any mental or physical handicaps.

I know she felt responsible for everything in my life that hadn't worked out–my divorces, my depression. She also felt that my brother's unhappiness was her fault as well as Carol's mental well being. She carried around a lot of guilt all her life. I told her she was a wonderful woman and that I loved her.

Mom continued to do those crossword puzzles right up until that day she went into the hospital. Even when she could no longer write, my sister would ask her for the answers and she would call out the words for Lisa to write them down. She was still sharp. Every time I pick up a newspaper now and turn to the puzzle section, I still find myself reaching for the scissors.

I set sail in my little boat
to find God.
I set out o'er the churning seas–
to find "The One"
who had called to me since birth.

It was a turbulent journey,
but I survived,
only to end up–
back on my homeland–
to find him there–
in your arms.

Chapter 5

Care For the Dying

I took my first trip home within the first few months, one of many that year. When I got there, she was so happy to see me. It had been a few years since I had been back, possibly three. Our relationship had taken on another form. I was now her supporter. Whatever she wanted, I would get for her. That was the least I could do for her. I loved her and wanted her to be comfortable. We laughed a lot, or I laughed a lot. Then mom finally caught on. I think at first, it almost felt unnatural to laugh so much, but I realized that I was happier in my life and naturally I laughed more.

This was new for her to see me this way. I'm sure she must have remembered me as the one who always had this sad, painful look on her face, never smiling, always looking like I was going to cry. From early childhood, I remember Mom saying, "Gail, would you smile a little? She even had a picture hanging in her parlor called "The Locket" that she liked a lot because it reminded her of me. It was of a very sad-faced little girl. But I wasn't that person anymore. Living so far away from each other, unfortunately, your only reminders are old pictures. So we laughed more those few days than we had laughed in years. She enjoyed it and started to look forward to it.

My nephews were being boys, especially the youngest, Bryan. Almost nine, he was devilish. He had that look in his eyes as though he were always doing something naughty, and he had the grin to prove it. He made his grandma laugh, and when he and I got together, I egged him on. It was pretty comical. The older one, Sean was more serious. He would have more difficulty dealing with Grandma's illness. He loved her and was very close to her; but her condition and the ultimate outcome was insurmountable to him.

I think he liked it when I came home to visit because there was always more laughter. My mom would say my name in such a sweet, reprimanding way at those times when I was egging Bryan on, leaving the boys with uncontrollable giggles. She'd try hard not to laugh, but couldn't help it, *"Gail! You are not helping this situation at all!"* She was so serious the first few times; but after that, she caught on. I know she enjoyed the bantering back and forth. As long as the boys giggled softly, it was acceptable. When she wasn't feeling well, she needed quiet.

We drove in search of turbans for her now hairless head. The town I grew up in was so small, there were very few specialty shops. There was a mall on the outskirts of town, but not even a movie theatre or a coffee house in town. So we drove far in search of turbans. Eventually, we found this salon that catered to cancer patients who had gone through chemotherapy. In the salon we found an *"earth angel."* That is the term I use for those people who are so filled with love and compassion for others, that they make us weep and remind us to open our hearts more. Their selfless care for the sick and dying is without a second thought. Their hearts are so full of love when they are near you that you feel it. It is an inspiration to know them.

It was an honor to know this woman and to be in her presence as though she were my mom's servant. She sat with my mom and spoke to her as if she were the center of the universe.

It was incredible to feel the emotions that I saw between them. Mom was feeling uncomfortable about losing her hair. I think for most women, hair represents how beautiful we are to others. We say it's not true, but that's how we feel about it. If we feel like we're having a "bad hair day" we feel ugly to others. I had also heard that we carry all of our emotions in our hair. All the old emotions we have ever felt or trauma sits in the hair. That's why when we have it cut, we feel so good; we are leaving behind or getting rid of all those attachments. A haircut gives us the feeling of freedom. We are a changed person.

So I believe that losing hair through chemotherapy for terminally ill cancer patients is part of the death process. We are losing some of the attachments and the identity we have held to. That identity is part of the ego and when we die, it is the death of that ego.

This earth angel brought out boxes of turbans and fit my mother. They talked color, fabric, texture, weight and seasonal changes. I could see in my mother's eyes how beautiful she felt, and I knew it had been a long time since she had felt this way. She lived such a solitary life. When she worked extremely hard, she slept on her days off. She had no social life and very rarely had visitors. She spoke with her friends on the telephone, but had very little physical contact with anyone except Lisa, who dedicated her life to our mother. She was my mother's lifeline to humanity. For the last year of my mother's life even though my sister had her own family and a full-time job an hour from home, even thought she lived ten miles from Mom, Lisa visited every day to care for her. The last few months of her life, Lisa would make the journey twice a day. That is what an earth angel does. And she never complained or thought for a moment that it was unfair or that she couldn't do it or didn't have the strength to go on.

My mother's dying taught me to look outside of myself more. These earth angels, in essence, changed my life. I saw them care for each other, care for the terminally ill, put their lives and their egos aside to do whatever it took to make that other human being feel loved and beautiful and touched. They say that when you are dying one of the biggest fears is that you are not beautiful enough to be received by God. I was told how important it was to physically touch the dying, touch their hands and their heads, to tell them how beautiful they are and that you love them so. They don't want you to be afraid of their dying body either. All the earth angels I encountered taught me how easy it was.

The woman in the salon, sat with Mom for quite a while, fitting her. We purchased four or five turbans. Mother walked out of the shop with a glow about her and a new turquoise paisley turban on her head. You would have thought she had won a million dollars. She was elated. From that day on, every time she left the house, she had a new turban on with her lipstick and her earrings. I loved her with no hair. She looked beautiful. My mom also had beautiful skin. There was hardly a wrinkle on her skin and she was sixty-four years old.

That trip was sweet. We always had steamed lobster at her home. That was our ritual every time I came home. It was Lisa's, Mom's and my favorite family meal. We spent sweet times together but never talked about the inevitable. It wasn't time. We were dealing with seeing each other for the first time in a few years and never spoke about the falling out, nor did we ever make any apologies. That was our pattern. There was never any "making-up." It was always left unsaid. When I left, we all cried. I was so afraid that I would never see her alive again.

I see each raindrop
as love
falling from heaven.
In each one–
I feel you calling to me.
"I love you! Come home to me,"
you say.

And I stand outside
under the rain–
as it falls from the sky,
looking up–
up into space–
breathlessly–
waiting!

I sent her a book on death and dying when I got back. It was "Embraced By the Light" by Betty J. Eadie. It was about a woman who had died in her hospital bed but had come back to life because it wasn't her time. It was about her journey to the other side and her experiences there. I thought it was a good time for Mom to read something on the subject so she wouldn't be afraid to die and she would know that it was safe and beautiful there. I also wrote her a long letter on my beliefs on death and dying.

I told her not to be afraid, that it was a beautiful place and she would be loved and well taken care of there. I told her the story about the soul being housed in the shell called the human body, until it was ready to be born into the spirit world of heaven. That was our true birth, not the human birth here as a baby and that the spirit birth (or death) was liberation for the spirit. This earth plane was a place we came to learn love and compassion before we were ready to be born.

I told her about the angels and all those who would be there with her, that it would be a celebration for her. The only emotion there is love, so there is no fear or sadness, only happiness and joy. You don't gasp for breath upon death. You will realize you can see, feel, hear, move, and breathe better than you could before. You will see everyone around you and you will be able to embrace those who are open and available to see you.

Your life doesn't pass before your eyes so that you experience all the pain you caused to others, as I had once been told. You view it all from a much higher, sweeter place of love and compassion. It is soft and sweet and easy and filled with peace. I so wanted her not to be afraid, to know like I did and to feel safe in the knowing that there was something out there that was so much more than all this. It was where we belonged and it was our first and original home.

When we spoke a few days after she received the book, she thanked me. *"Thank you for the book and the letter, Gail."* I said, *"Mom, some things are hard to speak about and this is one of them. I would probably cry and so would you, so I wrote it out instead. You know I was always better in writing than speaking with you face-to-face. I wanted you to know how I feel about this so you can understand it's okay. Let me know when you want to talk about it, okay?"* That was that; we never spoke about it again.

She knew I loved her and she knew I was there for her if she wanted to talk. We did over time, but in bits and pieces. I think this was normal under these circumstances. She told me that she wasn't afraid to die and that she would be ready when the time came. I watched as over those next few months she cleaned up and cleared out things in her life and put things in order. She was amazing. It wasn't just about her belongings or possessions. It was also putting things emotionally and mentally in order. When you are alive, you can have chaos in your life, but when you are preparing to die, you feel all the chaos has to be put in some kind of order for the passing.

Mom said she couldn't be bothered with people who hadn't been in touch with her, *"Let them go! I don't have time,"* she said. She was right. She didn't have a lot of time or energy to put into feeling sad or having regrets. It was time to forgive and let go. She hadn't spoken to her sister, in somewhere between one and two years. They had had a falling out on the telephone about something silly to us, but obviously not to them. I think when you have a history with someone, meaning you've shared a childhood, a family, a relationship of some sort, you see things differently. Every word or comment that comes out of his or her mouth means something far greater than it might seem to us. So if a sarcastic comment is made or a phone is hung up before a conversation is complete, it could mean, "*I'm disappointed in you!*" Then, the ego kicks in and emotions run high. The silent battle begins.

Mom loved her sister. She respected her and was proud of her for what she had accomplished in her life. Mom was a little jealous, I'm sure, of the travel and the excitement in Jeannette's life; but then again, who wouldn't be in mom's financial situation? She had struggled all her life without a husband, four children and no schooling or training to earn a living any other way but waitressing. Her sister, on the other hand, had never had to work and had a husband to support her and her children. He had passed away years ago and Jeannette was living comfortably still. Mom had tried to retire but had to go back to work because she couldn't afford to live on the social security she was entitled to. I don't think Jeannette ever knew these things. And I am sure they loved each other, but just couldn't get past whatever hurt and resentment was between them.

Mom also said she didn't want to be around people who felt sorry for her. If someone cried when they saw her, she'd get very nervous. When mom got nervous or frightened, her ego kicked in and she was that little girl with armor all about herself to protect her. She'd get tough like me. As I went through therapy, I would call it my *"warrior child"* mode. I was the brave little girl who could handle anything and everything that came my way . . . even the dragons and demons. I just realized that I got that from Mom. She'd cop this tough attitude and say something like, *"I don't need these people feeling sorry for me! If that's the way they are going to react, I don't need them and I don't want to see them! I don't have time for them."* She only wanted happy people around her now.

I understood completely. I had just had a dream and in it, my spirit guides had come before me to tell me that I had only three weeks to live. I wasn't scared or upset . . . just dismayed. I consciously remember in the dream that I had tried hard over these last twenty years to make a conscious effort to stay alive and to be very aware of wanting to live. I wasn't finished and there was so much more I wanted to do. I remember that when I was told in the dream that I had brain cancer, I held my breath so I could see if there was any pain to be felt. That was fear.

I made a list of all the things I wanted to do in the next three weeks, and all the people I wanted to hug and hold and tell them I loved them. At the top of my list was that I wanted to laugh every day. I came upon someone the first day, a good friend, who, when I told them of my cancer, cried and cried. I felt their pain, their sadness, their loss and I couldn't deal with it. It was overwhelming to me. I didn't want my last days to be filled with that type of emotion. So I told everyone that if they were going to be filled with sadness and weepy, I would not say good-bye to them. I lived through a few days in that dream and the thing that stuck out most was that every day, I belly-laughed. I remember how good it felt inside.

My human mind or ego was horrified when I awoke from that dream, shocked that I had that dream at all, but I remembered every deep emotion that I felt. Maybe the dream was a gift so that I could see and feel the experience from a dying person's perspective. In this way, I could support my mother more emotionally. So when Mom said she only wanted happy people in her life right now, I understood.

We were now talking about every three days on the telephone. We had some of the most wonderful conversations. She would share with me every conversation or encounter she had with friends, and all the little letters and cards she received. Most were so heart-felt that she would weep with me on the telephone. She told me about her wonderful friends who had been so thoughtful and giving to her. A few who knew how difficult it was to live on her fixed income would enclose a little cash for her. These were great gifts because they were so needed. But she would never let on how badly she needed help. She'd sometimes try to give the gifts back until she was told finally to *"keep them or else!"* It was very hard for Mom to accept anything from anyone else. She was proud, yes, but I think more than that, no one in her life had ever given her much of anything, except her children. Even with us, she was uncomfortable receiving gifts. Now she cherished everything she received with all her heart.

She shared with me her feeling that she had done the best job she could in raising us, and that she hoped we all found happiness and love in our lives. She said she loved her grandchildren and hoped they did well in life. She began giving me advice like a mom, and I listened to her like I had never listened to her before. I wanted more of the closeness–and although I knew my life was far away from hers–I yearned to be closer, to spend more time with her. I wanted to go to the beach with her or to dinner or shopping. I wanted to take her to the movies. I wanted to show her who I was as her daughter and who I had become as a woman and a mother. I knew now what a close, loving and healthy mother/daughter relationship was, and I yearned for it.

Your wide-eyed innocence stopped–
when you looked up at me.

And your open heart said,
"I love you, Mommy!"

Chapter 6

Angels In Waiting

There were a few more visits back home. On one, I took my son with me. He hadn't seen his grandma since he was six years old and now he was twelve. As we sat on the long plane ride, I remembered some of the old issues I had worked through. It was old *"stuff"* that had haunted me for most of my life. Although I had worked hard to release the painful memories of the last twenty years, I was still very conscious of them as I was preparing to take my own child back into my old childhood world. They were like pictures now instead of demons and I was playing them all out for review.

I had shared with my son some of my childhood memories and my relationship with my mother. So he was very aware of how I was feeling. He had a pretty healthy perspective on life and I enjoyed his young advice. For example, when I started to write this book, I was having difficulty gathering my thoughts and writing them down. At one point I was really struggling. He asked, *"Mom, why is this so difficult for you? It should just flow. It should be easy. If you fight it, it's not going to be any good at all so you might as well get up right now and walk away from it. Give it a rest!"* Out of the mouths of babes . . . .

He did well seeing his grandma. Prepared for how she looked, he hugged her. He also asked her a lot of questions. She enjoyed his wit and his mind. She was at peace and very content that he was there. Another grandchild and child had come home. The first night, Bryan slept over at Grandma's with

Troy. They didn't remember each other because they had both been so young during the last visit, so they were getting to know each other again. They bonded quickly, both having the same sense of humor. The house was filled with giggling laughter until they fell fast asleep exhausted. The next day, Sean came over and they all spent the day together. They got along so well considering they were three competitive boys.

I had not seen my brother in sixteen years or his thirteen-year old daughter, my niece. As it turned out that day, Mom got a call that she was in town from Maine visiting relatives. Mom was so happy that all her grandchildren would be together. That's all she had talked about lately. She was hoping for that miracle and it had come. Troy got a kick out of his boy cousins and this new girl-cousin, Hannah, from Maine, that faraway state. Hannah got a kick out of her Hollywood-looking cousin with the spiked hair, Troy from California. They had a blast together.

Unfortunately, Mom was not feeling well at all that day. I remember that it was the seventh day after her chemo and she was weak, but she wasn't going to miss this for anything. We went to my sister's house where we all sat on her deck while the kids played hide-n-go-seek and tag in her yard. We sat for hours as the weather held. Although it was early spring, it was warm outdoors. It was a day to remember. I treasured meeting Hannah, also an earth angel. My mother adored her. At that moment in time, I didn't think anything could top this day. It was so special for all of us.

The next day I drove Mom and the kids to Cape Cod. She talked about going to the beach the entire time she was ill. She wanted to be there so badly, needed to be there. Her soul was probably looking for that healing that is felt there in the sand at the water's edge. There always seemed to be a reason she couldn't get there. Either she was not feeling well enough or everyone was too busy and couldn't drive her. I asked her to come to the West and visit me but she was afraid of flying in an airplane. She had been to visit me twice since I had moved, but got more afraid of flying the older she got. Then her health was failing so quickly that she didn't have the strength to make the trip even if she had wanted to.

I know she did get to the beach a few times with Lisa, and I drove her twice. This day the boys played in the back seat as boys do. They laughed and giggled and tickled each other. Eventually they pushed the envelope with Mom. It was too much for her that day and she was not pleased. She didn't have the patience for them and wasn't very pleasant as she reprimanded them. Bryan, who doted on her, was nearly in tears. So I intervened and tickled his legs with my hand squeezed between the seats until he begged me to stop. I giggled right along with him and Mom said, *"Gail, you're not helping here."* I innocently said, *"What, mom? I'm not doing anything! Don't look at me!"* And then I'd wink and grin from ear to ear. Eventually, she broke down and started laughing, too.

Mom didn't sleep much that week I was there, even though she needed it. I know she was exhausted, but she wouldn't let on. I don't think she wanted to miss anything. She looked forward to the visits and knew I'd be going back to California much too soon. She hung in there the whole time I was there. On the last morning, my father called her. He wanted to see me. I'm sure he wanted to see her, too. Once he found out she was ill, he called her often to check up on her. It's funny . . . you couldn't have mentioned his name in front of my mother or had him in the same room with her for probably thirty-five to thirty-six years. Now he was calling her all the time and they were actually civil to each other. I hadn't seen my father in about thirty-five or thirty-six years except for about three or four hours and only one hour since I was in high school.

I had already forgiven him years ago for what he had done to me and for the things he hadn't done for me as a father. It was time to see him again before his passing. He had been almost as ill as my mother for the last year or so. He had emphysema (he was on a breathing machine), and severe osteoporosis (he had probably thirty cracks or fractures in his bones and later that year would be bedridden). He also had such poor circulation in his legs that they were ulcerative and the doctor had talked about amputation.

I learned so much from both my parents about how important it is to take care of our bodies. Both had smoked for over fifty years–and my father still smoked, even in the face of death. I also smoked for seventeen years, and only by the grace of God did I have the strength to stop at age thirty-one. I started again after that, smoking "socially" for a few more years until the dream. I dreamed one night that one of my spirit guides had come to me, and as we were standing on my balcony looking out over the horizon, he waved his arm. As he did, the view turned into a movie screen where I saw what would happen to my future if I continued to smoke. I awoke knowing that I would quit forever because of the fear of what I had seen. However, I cannot recall what I saw that frightened me so. I only remember the imprint it left.

I learned from my father what drinking does to the body and the soul. He never knew his children or had a life with us. I wonder what he remembers of his life? I wondered if he had any regrets? I never asked him. I wondered if I would get the chance before I finished this book? I heard somewhere that the reason alcoholics drink so heavily is to forget. They are so afraid to be alone with themselves–so afraid that they will be faced with who and what they truly are and will not be able to live with that. They are so afraid to stare themselves in the face that they have to drown that fear by numbing themselves.

It reminded me of the time I had come face-to-face with myself and had the anxiety attack. And it didn't happen just once. I can understand what it feels like to have to hide to survive. Sometimes that's all you can do. I try not to be judgmental on anyone because every time I am, I am faced with a similar issue, so that I feel that same emotion. I am shown another lesson in compassion.

That is how I forgave my father. Isn't it strange . . . you would think I would have had a harder time forgiving him for abandoning me when in fact it was my mother I was so hard on all my life. Puzzling.

It was now time for me to meet him as an adult and for my son to meet his grandfather for the first time. We met at my sister's house. An old friend of the family drove him over for an hour. We drove up at the same time and as we both got out of our cars, we walked over and hugged each other hard. He wept, *"I'm so sorry, Gail. I'm so sorry for everything. I'm sorry I haven't been there."* I interrupted him and said, *"Dad, that's not why I came here. I forgave you a long time ago."* So we both stopped talking and kept hugging. We cried and then walked into the house where my mother was and three of the four grandchildren that he had never seen.

"And she awoke from her long slumber,
she opened her eyes for the first time–
and noticed
how green the earth was . . ."

He hugged my mom and greeted the children. All at once, I felt like I wasn't an orphan anymore (a term I had used in jest, though it perfectly describes the feelings of my past family relationship). My mother, my father, my son, we had all come together in this place. My dad with his red cheeks was beautiful to me. He had always been very very tall (he was 6'7" when I was young) but now he seemed shorter than I remember at this stage in his life. An amazing hour was spent as he told how he had always loved my mother and that he somehow would like to take care of her for the rest of her life. He said they could take care of each other during their illnesses. He also admitted that my mom was his one true love and that she always was and always would be. That was strange, because Mom had told me the same thing just a few days before as we sat talking about her plight. It was the love story between my parents that was never meant to be–the one that most divorced children dream of. They dream, no matter how old, that one day, their family will be one again and everyone will be healthy and live happily together, forever after. But my father had been remarried for many, many years. And I couldn't forget that with the alcohol and the physical abuse, he and my mother were not destined to be together in this lifetime.

Dad told me stories of events in his life–of the time he had dinner with Elvis' manager and Priscilla. He had front row seats at the concert in Vegas and didn't think at the time what a big deal it was. Silly him, I thought. He also told me about how he loved God and that He was the most important thing in his life. He said he walked outside every day, talking to God and God talked back. He said he knew people would think him crazy for saying that, but he didn't care. He loved astrology and had a passion for things as he spoke. All these things fit and I realized how much like him I was. How incredible to be part of who he was! The rest of my "pieces of myself" finally fit. Now I knew where they came from. Life was so different now. But of course it would be. All those things that seemed so important to me before, no longer were.

That hour stretched on forever, or so it seemed. My mom sat quietly in the chair listening to all of us. She talked with him a bit, but I think it was probably a bit overwhelming for her after all these years. If it was such a heart-opening experience for me, can you imagine what it must have felt like for her? Every single event that happened during this trip was so special I would never forget it, nor would my son.

On that trip back, an old girlfriend from high school (a girl my mom disliked back then), came to visit when she heard Mom was ill. Mom had always felt she was a bad influence and had forbidden me to hang around with her in high school. We got into trouble by having boys over when we weren't supposed to. We lied about it. Of course we were innocents then and nothing happened, but I think she thought something could have happened, and she wanted to protect me. Debbie took us to dinner and we giggled and laughed for hours. She was like me in that sense. We had lobster, of course, and Mom had a ball.

The last night at my mom's, I slept on the couch with my nephew Bryan. I was having great difficulty going to sleep because I was worried about Mom. In the morning it would be time for me to leave. Restless, Bryan tossed and turned and slept with his eyes open, which was strange to me. I didn't know if he was looking at me, or if he was awake or sleeping. I could hear Mom's breathing in her bed and I was afraid she was going to die that night. I wanted to be there when it happened, but I was still afraid for it to happen. As I lay there with my eyes closed, aware of all the noises in the trailer, I could sense a lot of energy in the room. I opened my eyes and saw seven beings at the foot of my bed against the wall. They were standing in a row. I knew and sensed immediately that they were seven angels. I was told they were there for Mom and would be with her until her passing. I prayed to them that night that they would guide her and protect her and keep her from having any pain.

A funny thing happened the last month that Mom was alive. It was Sunday afternoon and I was home with my son. Lisa called to tell me she was having problems with her son, Bryan. He was afraid to sleep upstairs in his room, but he wouldn't tell her why. He had started to watch scary movies with his friends because it was cool, but she thought he had overdone it. Bryan was now sleeping beside his parents' bed on the floor. She put him on the telephone to talk with me. He hesitated at first and wouldn't tell me what was wrong, but then he said, *"Auntie Gail, I see dead people and I don't want to see them. They are scaring me."* It reminded me of a movie I had recently seen. I said, *"Bryan, so what do they want from you?" "I don't know, Auntie Gail. Do you think I would even ask? I don't want to see them at all. They're scaring me!"* He was panicked.

He continued to tell me that when he was at Grandma's house the other night, he had seen seven men in white robes and really long white beards all lined up against the wall in her living room at the foot of the couch. I laughed and said, *"Bryan, those are the seven angels that are with Grandma until she passes over. They are going to guide her and protect her. It's okay. They won't hurt you. You can pray to them."*

"Why would I want to do that?" Bryan asked. I could tell he was relieved. He said, *"I don't even want to see them. I want them to go away when I am there."* So I gave him the prayer I taught my son: *"In the name of the divine father and mother, to those of you who are present in this room or in this house. I command that you leave here if you are not in the white light of God. You are not welcome here. Only those that are of the Divine Father are welcome in my home."*

He slept in his own bed that night and every night thereafter.

It was harder to leave mom at the end of this trip. I cried because I didn't know if I'd see her alive again. My life had changed so much from the meeting with Hannah, my niece, and my father, my son's reunion with the family and my mother. This trip had changed my life. It had been changing so much in this past year. I no longer felt like the little girl with no father or mother. I belonged somewhere to someone who loved me and now I was grown up enough to let the mask or the ego down enough to feel it. To me, it seemed, I had met my father for the first time. My fractured family was finally healing.

Chapter 7

Grief At Twilight

After I left this last time, Mom and I knew it would be a few months before I got back again. I would have to start playing financial catch-up for all those past trips. This coupled with the chemotherapy coming to an end, began to depress her. As time went on, she realized her energy level was getting worse instead of better. She was becoming weaker. Her days consisted of getting out of bed, feeding her cat and dog, having breakfast, doing a load of laundry, sitting in the chair, napping for energy, getting up, feeding everyone again, sitting in the chair and going to bed. Occasionally, she would have a visitor, go to the grocery store with my sister when she was up to it, or go to her numerous doctor appointments or therapy. She led a pretty quiet life. None of this changed after she found out she had cancer.

She called to tell me how depressed she was. She thought she would have more strength and energy and that she would be on the mend. I think she truly thought a miracle would happen and she would be cured. The reality of her situation was setting in again. She was also so winded all of the time. An inhaler helped somewhat, but just walking across her small kitchen left her breathless.

I kept sending her puzzles and cards and small treasures. I sent her my special prayer beads that had been blessed. Someone very dear to me had made them for me. I told Mom how much they meant to me and that I loved her so much, I wanted her to have them. I sent her a carved rose quartz heart with a message about being loved so much. But her depression seemed to continue. The smallest things lifted her spirits. If one of her grandchildren had a game and did well, that became the most important thing to her and brought her a very happy moment. If a friend from far away called to talk with her or sent a card, she was effusive about what they said. Even a trip to the local grocery store was important to her day and always lifted her spirits. But it was getting harder to keep them lifted.

Her life seemed so simple to me. I had always busied myself with little tasks and events and appointments. In this way, I never stopped just to "be". I wouldn't have to stop and be in the moment or find happiness where there was nothing to fill my time. My mother had mastered this in her simple life. I would have been deeply depressed with all those open spaces where any thoughts could creep in. And what would be so frightening? What thoughts or feelings would come in that I feared? Maybe something from my childhood . . . a memory perhaps? Maybe facing myself, you know, the "self-love" thing. I never would have survived living like her. Most of my life I couldn't face myself alone. I was too afraid of what I would learn about myself. I could be a "bad" person. I could be someone so yucky that no one would want to love me and then I would be "found out."

Mom had mastered this in her life. She was who she was. Her life was what it was. It was simple. There were no frills or anything fancy about it. It was black and white. She loved everyone and she knew who she was. If they didn't like her, then too bad. She wasn't afraid of what people thought of her. She wasn't afraid to face herself. She sat at her kitchen table every day for hours and faced herself. I didn't learn this until this month in her life. It was profound.

HOW BRILLIANT!

That we have created this lifetime with all its

CHAOS–

our busy work schedules–
and little "appointments"

that
run
into
each
other. . .

We are so caught up playing the
Game of Life
That we have forgotten the
Meaning of Life.

The weeks went on and I started calling every other day, with stories of my work, my days with my son, my dating, my dreams, my life. I realized that she looked forward to all those stories and wanted so much to hear and know more. She offered advice as a mother and laughed with me or got angry if someone wasn't very nice to my son or me. It could be something as small as a negative response to a question we asked or an argument between my son and a friend of his. She was being protective, and supportive.

I had told her in detail about someone I had been dating for quite some time. I was ending the relationship because I was ready for more of a commitment and he had made it very clear that he could not offer me any more than he already had. I had struggled for years, because I had fallen in love with him. He lived in another state and came to the coast once a month to see me. I had allowed my heart to be broken too many times and again was struggling with this one.

I hadn't seen him in months and got a phone call one weekend. I had been weeping all weekend, grieving the eventual passing of my mother as I so often did lately. The message was, *"Gail, I'm sitting on my balcony in Pacific Beach, looking at the waves and waiting for the sun to fall into the ocean. It's beautiful. If you jump into your car right now, you can be here in time to watch the sunset with me. I know you've been going through a lot with your mom, and I want to support you as best I can. Please come."* For a moment, my ego went, *"But, but he broke my heart! He hurt me! I am not going!"* Then my heart wept and I realized I wanted so badly to be held.

So I went. We sat on the balcony overlooking the ocean, watching the sun fall into the water. And then we went to dinner. We returned and sat until well after midnight as we watched the moon also fall into the water. I had never before sat long enough to see the sun set and the moon rise through the sky and then set in the same place as the sun. It was an incredible experience. We talked and I cried. It was so nice to be with him again. He had such a sweet and loving heart when he allowed me to see it. We walked on the sand for hours before I returned to my reality. It was very healing.

The next afternoon, I called Mom. She was deeply depressed as she had been so often lately. I shared this story with her and she was enraptured. She said, *"Gail. That sounds wonderful. How beautiful. You need to get out and enjoy yourself more often. That was so thoughtful of him to call you.*

You know he cares about you. I'm so glad you went!" She sounded excited. You would have thought she was the one who had gone down to the ocean instead of me. She loved the ocean as I did and I'm sure it seemed romantic to her.

Her depression set in that day when she received a letter from the state telling her that they would be talking $35.00 per month out of her now meager check to pay for her health insurance. She had been struggling financially all her life, and even in death she would struggle. It was a kick in the teeth when she was down. I was very worried about her depression this time because I actually feared she might contemplate suicide. She even mentioned the word to me. I decided it was time to make another trip home. I was worried about her mental and emotional state now. I was so torn up inside with such guilt and yearning to be closer, to hold her hand and take care of her. How was I going to survive through all of this? Would I be there in time?

When I told her I was coming, she of course said, *"Gail, don't waste your money! You don't have to come. I'm fine."* But I said, *"Mom, it's our birthday month. This is my gift to you. We'll all have lobster at home to celebrate our birthdays. No presents, just lobster. OK? I'll be there in four weeks."* So she agreed and gave me her blessing. I called the airlines and called my sister Lisa to let her know how concerned I was with mom's depression. My sister had already started dropping by twice a day to care for Mom so she was aware of the frequent changes in her moods.

I think Mom was starting to feel her body slipping away from her, which meant she wouldn't be in control of it any longer. This is probably a big fear for the elderly. No one wants to have to rely on others for all their needs. This is humiliating and frustrating. There is no dignity in it because we were meant to be kings and queens of our lives and our destiny. That's what we strive for in life. So when control slips away from us it feels like we have failed. If I were the one with cancer, I would have taken my own life so long ago. I wouldn't have had the strength my mother had to stay with it through these long months.

My sister and I tried to find agencies to help with mom's financial crisis. She finally found someone to help and was able to get $200.00 more a month, but Mom would never live to see it. There was a sixty-day waiting period, during which time Mom would pass away. This and the news that I would be there in a few more weeks, helped lift her spirits once again. He birthday was also around the corner.

It was getting harder and harder to be away from her. I doubted myself as a daughter and was slipping in and out of depression, also. It was starting to affect my relationship with my son. I was very impatient with him and we began to argue more. Sometimes he would catch me weeping. He was confused and so was I. I was no longer focused at my work, which affected my projects and the department I managed.

The amazing thing about this whole experience was that I had such an inner strength and belief system. I knew where we came from and where we would go after this place. I loved meditating on, contemplating, reading, studying, and hearing people talk about death and the "other side." It was the destination I have always looked forward to at the end of my life. Maybe it was the memories from my childhood as my body slept and my spirit soared with the angels and Mother Mary. And maybe it was that deep "inner knowing" that made me feel wrapped up safe inside the wings of the angels when I called them forth. I knew what was waiting there for me—love. Unconditional and divine love.

Nevertheless, I still wept and grieved and suffered with depression. I thought it would be so much easier than this.

Since I felt I knew so much, and since my mom's whole life had been such a struggle, I felt the afterlife would be a better place to go. She would be in a place I myself had waited patiently and anxiously to embrace. Knowing all this still didn't make it any easier. Death and dying represents the death and the dying of the human bond with another, no matter how deep the love between us is. It is sorrow and pain and sadness for our loss. Grief is the feeling we feel when we realize that the relationship and the connection will be broken when our loved one passes through the veil and we stay behind. Our lives will no longer be touched, enriched, or moved by them. I realized that each time someone dies, those of us left behind as humans come one step closer to our destiny. Our hearts are opened and expanded a little more with each passing and our souls are forever imprinted. But still, knowing all of this with the mind does not prepare the heart for what is to be felt. If we knew ahead of time, the experience wouldn't be the same or have the same impact on us. The whole experience teaches us love and compassion.

Still I grieved and cried like everyone else, regardless of the differences in our beliefs about death and dying and the other side. My whole life and all the choices I had made were flashing before my eyes. They say that the dying, just before they pass, begin reviewing their lives. I was also doing a review. I was reliving every decision I had ever made regarding my family, my life on the east coast, my relationships and my life here. It was a very long process. Every waking moment I was processing all of it. I was weeping, grieving, questioning. I was very confused. I was also having dreams that I was also dying. I felt that I was my mom, that somehow, we were one and the same. I needed to be there with her. How would I keep my job and do this? I wanted to be there. I awoke every morning and went to sleep every night with these thoughts.

Within a few weeks, my sister called with more news on Mom's condition. The cancer had spread to the brain (which we had known) but now was spreading rapidly. Her doctor was recommending radiation every day for a period of time. Also, they wanted to start her on steroids. These treatments would help her with the pressure and the pain from the growth and would make her more comfortable for a while.

It seems that when a disease of this magnitude takes over the body, the medical profession wants to extend the life of the patient. After all, they have been trained to save lives. This is okay if the patient wishes his life to be extended, but I'm not sure it's the best choice at times. Mom did better than most with the chemotherapy, but there were still more side effects that were harder on her then the cancer itself. Her life was extended a great deal, but at times, she was so ill, she had no quality of life. I know Mom heard her oncologist tell her that it was small-celled cancer and was incurable, but toward the end, she asked me and the doctor why they even bothered to do the chemo anyway. The doctor told her that it had extended her life so that she could get her affairs in order and it had. If she had not had the chemo, she wouldn't be sitting there in her office ten months later.

Her oncologist was an earth angel who had dedicated her life to cancer and the treatment and care for cancer patients. My mother loved and trusted her and we did, also. She had a heart as big as her list of patients. We trusted her completely so we agreed to the radiation treatments. Mom was also beginning to become more disoriented. She was still doing her crossword puzzles every day, and said, "*Thank you, Gail for the puzzles. They keep my mind sharp.*" She was amazing. Sometimes she couldn't find the words for something she was trying to convey to us, but sometimes she was sharp as a tack, remembering every minute detail.

Around this time or shortly before the radiation treatments started, she began slurring her words like she was drunk. We thought she had a stroke and Lisa immediately got her to the doctors. It was not a stroke, but the cancer in the brain. It would come and go. She had beautiful handwriting, but now she could not write legibly.

During this time, I noticed and savored all the special things about Mom that had been a part of her throughout her life. Her handwriting was beautiful and fluid. She had beautiful blue eyes that everyone commented on. I loved her nose. It was a little larger than most with a little crookedness to it and a faint scar across the bridge. I remember when she fell down the stairs and got that scar. I remember when she was lying in the hospital at the end while I rubbed her feet, hands and head with lotion. She had the longest fingers and the most elegant hands and feet. She saw the calluses and the bunions when she looked down at her feet. I saw those long elegant feet that my sister and I had inherited from her.

She devoured her crossword puzzles–something I also loved to do–and she loved a cup of tea with her toast. She would talk to herself and her animals when she was alone, as if they were human beings. I admired the simplicity in her life. She found beauty in the smallest of things, while I was always searching or reaching beyond. She was content in her life and in herself. Mom carried herself as though she were royalty. Knowing of our family problems and where her life had taken her, I never understood where that feeling came from inside of her. But I admired it. She held her head high. And when she smiled, the room lit up. All of these special qualities were coming to me with every visit and every phone call. She was my mother.

As we lived through the radiation with her, we knew she was beginning to fail. Her blood pressure was dangerously high so they tried to control it with medication. They were treating her as if she were a diabetic. The steroids made her face swell until it was frighteningly big and round. She called me, crying; she was so confused and upset with the way she looked. It frightened her when she looked in the mirror. I cried with her, for her and for me. I wanted to be there to hold her hand and to hug her and take her pain away.

I prayed for her every chance I got during every day, in the car, in bed, at work. I lit candles for her continually; my faith was so strong. I begged that she would not be in any pain and that she would make peace with everyone and everything in her life so she could go home to God. And miraculously, she was not in much pain. By the grace of God, she was saved the pain. I was not sure she would tell us if she was in pain anyway.

Those two weeks of radiation were so long. Many times I stayed awake all night with insomnia. She began to have trouble moving physically. She could sit down and lie down, but now she couldn't raise herself up from those positions. Everything was so intermittent and nothing was consistent. She wouldn't hear of hospice coming in to her home or maybe the possibility of moving somewhere else. She did not want to leave her home and her beloved animals.

My brother-in-law began to install handicapped features throughout her trailer and special chairs that were high enough so she could raise herself up. My sister was calling me more and breaking down on the telephone. She was struggling emotionally. I was very concerned that she couldn't keep up this pace. It was so hard on her because she was mom's baby and she loved her so much. She had to go by in the morning and get mom out of bed, bring her to the bathroom, and then sit her up in the chair. Someone would come by in the middle of the day and Lisa would come back at night to sit with her and then put her to bed. Once Mom was down, she couldn't get up.

Each day I called, she'd tell me she was fine. She explained in specific detail what her symptoms and problems were, but also that she was absolutely fine. One day, we talked about Hospice. I was due home the following week. She said, *"Yes, I think we need to talk but let's wait until you get here. We can talk about a lot of things then."* Excited, she was waiting for me to come to her.

After talking to her, I hung up the receiver and cried and cried. I was so sad, so overwhelmed and feeling so helpless. I needed to be there now. I couldn't wait another week. Each time I talked with her over the next few days, she tried to sound so upbeat, but I knew she was fading fast. I could feel it in her voice and in her spirit. She was struggling. We all were. Lisa was now there constantly and this was taking a toll on her children. Both boys were missing their mom and Bryan was especially having difficulty. Now I lay in bed each night thinking about Mom.

The angels–
heed your prayers, and
carry them to God
upon their wings.

There,
they kiss each one
gently,
and offer them up to him.

Chapter 8

"I'm Coming, Mommy!"

I was due to fly out on Saturday morning and it was only Monday. Around mid-day, I called her to wish her a happy birthday. Although she was happy to hear from me, she sounded more confused. She was almost giggly as we chatted. She was so excited that I would be there in five more days. She always thought she would die very young like her mom, so she was surprised that she had made it to sixty-five.

For her birthday, my brother-in-law had sent her a large bouquet of roses and brought three lobsters. But she would never touch the lobsters–on that day, or any day after that. She wasn't in the mood to eat anything at all. We talked for about five or ten minutes and she told me she had to take a nap. It seemed she was on a cloud somewhere. There wasn't any emotion, maybe a little elation. It was hard to put my finger on. She said, *"Gail, I'm so tired. I'm lying down and have to go now to take my nap. I love you."*

This was the first time she didn't want to spend time talking with me. I was concerned and spoke with my sister. She seemed dazed also, and I sensed things were not going well. I called later and Lisa said Mom was in bed. The next day when I called, Lisa said she was sleeping again. I called a few times on Tuesday and she was in bed sleeping every time. Lisa was a mess emotionally, as though she also was fading away. I think she felt helpless and didn't know quite what to do except to be there. I needed to be there for her, too. I knew I had to go now. I didn't sleep at all that night.

On Wednesday, I drove into work and tried to focus but couldn't. Two other managers came into my office with a problem and I burst into tears. I couldn't hold it in any longer. After explaining what was happening, one of them took my ticket and went about seeing what he or the company could do to get me on an earlier flight. There was so much concern. I couldn't remember anything that was said to me. It was 10:00 a.m. when I fell apart and knew I had to leave before it was too late. I was not fully and consciously at my work from that point on. I was grieving heavily and nothing made sense to me; I couldn't even put thoughts or words together. It was amazing that I made the hour-long drive home.

My friends and my ex-husband came to my rescue and took charge immediately. My son would stay with his dad while I was away. A friend came over that afternoon to write down what needed to be taken care of at my home, including my pets and another friend drove me to the airport to catch a red-eye out of Los Angeles. They were my earth angels and special friends. I had always kept all of them at a distance until this experience, never allowing them to come too close when I was blue. I would "hole-up" in my home alone, sad, knowing that I was that little warrior that could handle everything on my own.

For me, it was a fear of loving so much and feeling so deeply touched by another that I would break.

Love beyond life–
Too deep to feel
with the human heart.

To be touched
with such emotional passion–
would surely shatter our bodies
like a crystal egg that had been dropped
upon a granite floor.

During the last days of Mom's life, my heart began to open and I began to experience deep, deep love. It was the feeling of being loved by others and of loving others more deeply than you would ever have thought you could. It was painful at first. and I was fearful. But after a time of being in that expanded moment of feeling so deeply, it was no longer unbearable. It was like being bathed in white light. It was the feeling I get when I pray deeply with my heart and come out of my meditations. It was that feeling of being wrapped up inside the arms of the divine.

I welcomed everyone with an open heart from that point on. I was no longer afraid. I thank my mother for giving me the gift of life, but especially the gift of this experience. I would have missed out on one of the most important events of my life had I not come to her. I came away from all of this knowing that this was the most important thing I would ever do in my life, ever accomplish. It was my whole purpose. After Mom passed, I told my sister, *"If I die tomorrow, this was why I have lived. This was my whole purpose in life."* Another glorious gift . . .

That Wednesday, September 20th, two days after Mom's birthday, was another awakening. It was 10:00 a.m. when I broke down and it was 11:00 a.m. when I tried to track Mom, my sister and my brother-in-law down by phone. I finally got Glenn on his cell phone. He said, *"Gail, it doesn't look good. I just carried her into the hospital. You had better come now."* Then he broke down. It amazed me that my intuition–or a deeper connection with Mom–had told me at that moment that she had made some type of decision to take the next step in her rebirth process. I never questioned the powers that be. I just knew and now accepted what was happening.

On the long plane ride I reviewed my life with my mother and our relationship over the years. Every conversation, every interaction, every emotion that we ever shared came flooding back. Not all were good, either. But I somehow got through the guilt and was able to see everything in a new light, with no judgment. all had served a purpose. I firmly believe that Mom had dedicated her life to me to change me and grow me into a loving, compassionate woman who was not afraid to open her heart and give and receive divine love. I thought about everything that I had resented or disagreed with and saw each with its purpose or intent. I saw what I had learned. And I wept, knowing that this was another gift from her.

I arrived at the hospital at 8:30 a.m. No one was there yet, so I dropped my suitcase and ran to the bed. I hugged her and held her. She was so surprised and so happy that I was there, that she tried to speak, but she couldn't. It was a bad day and she couldn't put words together, so she couldn't speak at all. The words ran into each other, rhyming and then changing into meaningless sounds. She was frustrated and the tears ran down her cheeks. I held her hands all morning so that she would know I was with her. I was so full of emotion. Physically, she was not doing well. It was the ugliest day I had seen so far. The cancer was ravaging her body. Funny I should choose that word. When Mom was in for her chemo, the nurses would ask her how she was doing that day and she would say, *"I'm ugly today. Really ugly!"* They got a kick out of that.

She lay there coughing up matter from her lungs all that day. Embarrassed, but also fearful that she would choke to death and not be able to catch a breath. Because she was in more pain, we began a light morphine drip to help her. She wanted to be fully conscious and that was also what we wanted for her. That night, the nurses came in often to suction her out so she wouldn't choke. It was a lost day for all of us and I thought we would lose her then. It was difficult to see her lying there quietly. I knew that in her mind she didn't want to be a bother to anyone. Mom would never ask for anything or allow anyone to care for her. That was not her. I am sure this was hard, but at the same time, having Lisa and I there loving her meant the world to her. She told those close to her that she did not want to die alone. And she didn't. She threw a party.

Her wonderful doctor came in and told us that she had developed an acute blood infection and that the cancer had moved into her bone marrow. Also, her immune system had shut down and she was running a very high fever. There were so many complications. They were still treating her with steroids and other medications for her blood pressure and blood sugar levels, and now they added the morphine and some sort of aspirin for her fever. There was a stream of earth angels in and out of her room constantly. There seemed to be a new nurse or caregiver who came in every thirty minutes to check on her or to administer something. I had no idea until the last day that we were in ICU.

All the angels had smiles on their faces and they all touched mom's hands or arms. They made sure they touched her, I noticed. I was so impressed with this because I had learned that when a human being is dying, touch from others is so important. It lets the patient know he or she is loved and worthy of being touched. Touching them and holding them and telling them you love them, in effect lets them know they are beautiful and worthy and special and loved. I wondered if they were trained to do that or if they just "knew" to do it? They all had huge hearts. When they saw our tears or the tears in Mom's eyes, their eyes welled up as well. What a heart-wrenching job to care for the dying and their families day after day.

On her second day in the hospital, that day I arrived, was the worst, believe it or not. Each day after that, as she came closer to going "home" she became happier and more alive. It was an incredible thing to watch. It was as if her heart were singing because she "knew."

My soul is filled with life!
It wants to sing
every moment–
it comes closer to you!

It knows you–
when you pass by,
for it feels your pull,
and your kisses upon my heart.

Chapter 9

The Blanket

My sister Lisa wasn't holding up so well on this day, Thursday. She was exhausted both physically and emotionally. She also couldn't deal with the physical aspects of Mom's condition that day and it was understandable. I too was exhausted. Sleeping next to Mom that night, I was probably up and down every fifteen minutes or so to sit with her whenever I heard her coughing or moaning. I was living on caffeine and in that surreal state. I wanted to make sure I was there for her every moment. That was the least I could do for her and my sister who had carried the burden for so long. I told Lisa to go home and sleep with her family that night, that I would stay and call her if there were any changes at all. I also wanted time to be alone with my mom. Even if she couldn't speak, it didn't matter. I wanted to be close.

The second day was a glorious one! She awoke with her speech and she was very conscious. She was able to speak with everyone that came in and there was a crowd that came to visit. The nurses that treated her during her chemo and radiation came to visit that day. They said she was a bright spot in their days. Their hearts lay open each day as they worked to care for the dying. They were like empaths, feeling the patient's pain and the family's as well as their own compassion. I am sure it was not easy.

They related stories to my sister and me of the times Mom would come in for treatment and leave them in stitches. If she wasn't feeling "ugly" she cracked jokes and teased them until they couldn't stop laughing. She told each one of them, *"Don't think you are going to forget about me when I'm gone. When you look up in the corner of the room and see a speck of dust, that's me. So don't brush me down."*

There was a lot of emotion that day that went from one end of the spectrum to the other. We cried and felt our hearts heavy and full. But as we felt we couldn't take any more pain, she cracked a joke or said something hysterical. We belly-laughed quite a few times that day. She was very aware of what she was doing and saying. It was almost as if her mission was to make this as easy as possible for all of us.

When a parent is dying, your physical body and emotional body switch to autopilot. You aren't really sure what you are doing, where you are going next or even what has happened in the last few hours. You have very little recall and can see and feel only where you are in each moment. The moment is all that is important. For that reason, I am so thankful to my brother-in-law, Glenn that he was there. Lisa and I were like two little girls who couldn't make any decisions. We were so caught up in the moment, we didn't even think to call our siblings or other relatives. Glenn took control and told us we should make some calls. He also made all the calls to the long-distance relatives–some of them difficult to track down. Mom had misplaced her address book, or maybe we had lost it. Nevertheless, we were missing some phone numbers.

Glenn called my brother Steven. I hadn't seen him in sixteen years. He hadn't spoken to Mom in quite a while. Lisa and I weren't going to call anyone. We assumed that everyone would know somehow, and that if they wanted to come or thought it was important, they would be there. We didn't realize how important it was for the relatives to get that final phone call so they could make the final decision to make peace with themselves and Mom, or not.

I got paged to the nurse's station sometime later that day and it was my brother. He demanded to know what was going on and how bad it was. I told him it was bad and he needed to come now. It didn't sink in for him until I said, *"Steven, she is dying. It will probably be today or tomorrow. If you want to come, you had better come right now."* I think he was in shock and denial. But it finally sunk in, and he came. He lived eight hours away by car, so he napped for a few hours and was there within the next twelve hours, along with his wife and child.

I thought about my older sister, Carol. Mentally and emotionally handicapped, she had always disappeared when there were problems. She could not deal with high emotions or chaos. She could not deal with Mom being ill. On my first trip home after it was announced, she left within a few days because she couldn't deal with it. I thought that if we called her to pick her up and bring her to the hospital, she would disappear before we got there. I didn't have the time for that. But I did call her and Glenn went to pick her up in the town she lived in forty miles away. Often in times of crisis, when someone came to get Carol at her apartment, she wasn't there. We were not surprised. Carol was a little girl of about ten most of the time. She was also very nervous and forgetful. She had been so nervous after she got my call that she had called a friend who had driven her immediately to the hospital. Poor Glenn had gone all that way for nothing, but at least Carol was with us now.

Carol was an emotional mess when she came in to see Mom, so I made sure to keep an eye on her for the rest of the duration. It was again my responsibility as her "big" sister since Mom was dying. When I was young, I felt responsible for raising all of them while Mom was working. I was the responsible one now. I felt I had to make sure my younger brother and younger sister were okay during the day. Now, as we stayed at the hospital, I would watch that role play itself over and over again. I believe I wanted to be in charge so that I could feel in control of my life in those last days.

I don't remember calling cousins Bob or Roy or Kathy. I think someone else must have. Or maybe I did call. I don't remember. Bob and Kathy were my mom's age and had grown up with her. They had even lived with my grammy and grampy in the same house with us for a time with their mom, my grammy's sister. I hadn't know these details until now, however. Bob told us stories of Mom when she was a teenager and how much fun she had been. He said she always stuck up for him when he got into trouble. He laughed as he recalled some of the sweet memories they had shared. Kathy had shared a few, too. It was a part of mom's life I never knew.

Roy came with his wife and daughter. They loved Mom, and although they lived in Maryland, they got in their car and drove up immediately and were at the hospital within the next twelve hours. Roy was Mom's sister's son. Jeannette and Mom hadn't spoken in a long while and she still chose not to come. We didn't know what the "falling out" was about, probably something silly to us, but her choice was made. Sometimes life happens just the way you make it. I felt bad, because I knew she would grieve after mom's passing.

This was what it was like to be family, I realized. When there is a crisis, everyone shows up. For whatever reason you come–whether it be personal, for grieving or fear, or for support– just being there is what family does. This was the first time in my forty-six years that I had experienced that feeling or had been part of something like this. Maybe it was because I had let my ego rule my life and my choices in this arena. I had closed myself off from my family for twenty-one years. I had never been in the presence of this kind of commitment before. I was in awe of the love and support that was in the room with Mom. There was so much undying and constant love. It took this experience to show me the value of family.

In my life I had never really touched my mom, either. It had always been a policy of *"not speaking about the bad things"* all our lives. We just didn't hug or touch each other, so I didn't know how. We had never been a hugging family. When I had moved to California about the time of my marriage, a girlfriend was leaving my home after dinner. She wrapped her arms around me for a hug and I thought I had hugged her in return. She said, *"You know, Gail, you never hugged much as a child, did you? We need to teach you how to hug."* Then she laughed. I laughed, too, but never forgot that comment. I have learned how to hug sincerely and deeply since then.

Now I touched Mom, held her hands and rubbed her feet and her body–from the moment I arrived until hours after her death. To me, I think I was making up for my whole life of not touching her. It was my way of showing her how much I loved her. I wanted to make sure she knew I was there for her and that I would never leave here during this time. I also felt that touching the body was a way of saying *"I love you."*

All her friends from town came to see her that day. It was a miracle when she awoke; her speech was clear and concise, and she was fully conscious, and very much alive. She joked with us and giggled and made us laugh all day. It was one big party. We cried, but she would have us laughing in no time as though her entire agenda for the day was to show us how to laugh in the face of grief and sadness. I personally felt that the powers that be (God, spirit) gave her the voice and the will that day to greet people, to say her good-byes and to share with us her journey to the other side.

All of my life I have had great love and devotion for God or Spirit, even though I had never been able to understand or remember until I got much older. My idea of divinity changed into many forms as the years passed and I researched many different religions, yet the feeling was always the same. I had read, studied and researched a lot about death and dying. I was always so intrigued with what it was all about, and had realized it was probably triggered by my childhood dreams. But I had never been in the presence of someone passing over in the way my mother had chosen to pass.

On that second day, she talked to everyone and hugged and held them as they wept. She made it perfectly clear that she did not want anyone in that room crying. So they stopped. As she was reviewing her life, she would share little stories of things that had happened to her. She reminded Bob and Kathy of things they had done together when they were younger. I was learning about her life now. She was so animated. She reminded me of a queen with her court, sitting there so regally in her bed. All of her "*people*" were surrounding her, waiting for her to speak her pearls of wisdom, as if they would be her last words. She was so different from what I had ever known her to be.

Mom began to tire about mid-day and drift in and out of sleep. She had never really slept for the last few days, but catnapped instead. Or perhaps she had just closed her eyes for a few minutes at a time to go to the other place. The miracle of it was that when she went there, she shared with us what was happening. I truly believe that there are absolutely no mistakes in this life and that every single event has a purpose. I think the purpose of all this was to bring my family together, to give us new hope, and to change each of our lives. That it did.

All of that day, Lisa, Carol and I sat on Mom's bed holding

her hands. There were three of us and only two hands, so we moved continually to have equal touching time with her. Carol held up well most of the time, as long as Lisa and I did. Being the baby of the family, Lisa was struggling. She was the daughter that all moms would want as their own. She was an earth angel, as also were her children. She gave innocently from the heart in all things. My mom and Lisa had the relationship that I had always wanted with her. I grieved that fact in her passing, because I had not had the courage to take the chance with her. I had missed out.

My brother also came that day with his family. He walked cautiously toward the bed and when Mom opened her eyes, they both held each other and started to cry. I think he said something like, "*I'm so sorry, mom. I love you so much.*" I think her response was, "*Steven, I love you. There's nothing to be sorry for.*" Her baby boy had come home. They both melted into each other's hugs and tears until our world was back in one peace that day.

Our tears that day were not only for sadness and loss, but also for happiness and joy and every other emotion you could possibly express as a human being. We were so raw–perhaps like little babies with no clothes on, who had been lying in the sunshine long after our skin was burned, waiting for the next learning experience, or for someone to come. We couldn't be saved until we had experienced it all.

Sometimes, I think the reason some of our loved ones choose to leave this world with a long suffering illness that takes its toll on everyone's heart, is to heal the fractured family. Our family was so fractured that we would have stayed that way forever. She was a great saint and an angel for doing this for all of us. And she did not leave until all of her work was done.

Did you know that
relationships –
are meant to teach us
how to love ourselves?

As she drifted in and out of sleep, we heard every word she uttered or whispered about what was taking place in the other world. I started to write her words down out of nervousness, but Lisa became so enraptured by some of the things she heard that she kept asking me, *"Did you get that? Did you write it down?"* It became very healing to all of us to walk outside the room when the caregivers were tending to her, and discuss what she had said.

The second day of her stay, she began to talk about painting the ceiling and the walls. Over the next few days, the different colors she mentioned would tell us of her progress. She'd finish one color and say, *"Oh, Gail. I don't like this one."* So she'd start again. In the beginning, she was alone, but after the first few colors, she was painting with friends and loved ones or with her dog, Red who finished the last lilac or lavender color with her.

Her journey had begun here on earth with the world wars. As she had moved from the Japanese camps to the German camps, she began talking about the horrors she had seen. As she talked, she seemed to be participating in all of them, experiencing the torturing and the bombing. She seemed to be suffering each emotion that came up for the prisoners as well as the tormentors. You could hear the horror and emotion in her voice as she talked to the other soldiers. She was now viewing the scenes and feeling them from a higher place. You could hear the sorrow and the compassion in her voice. She was begging everyone to see it from her new perspective.

She talked about having to get to the ninth level before she could complete her transition. Each level was a plane of review and learning for her. We could hear bits of conversation with those she met on each level, some of the learning that was taking place, and her emotions as she experienced all of it. She never experienced any pain or sadness, only love and happiness. Only once did she feel fear, and it was about having to give up her "blanket." The blanket represented something weighty to Mom. She held it tightly to her heart and as "they" (whoever they were on the other side) tried to take it from her, she almost cried out, *"It hurts, Gail. Why does it hurt so badly? I can't breathe! It's so heavy!"*

"What, mom? What is so heavy?"

"My blanket. They want to take it away from me! Please don't let them!"

She held her fists tightly to her chest as though she were holding onto something. I said, *"Mom, if you don't want to give up the blanket, you don't have to. You can keep it."* She finally relaxed and fell asleep for a while. The blanket represented something more than we knew. She said she couldn't move on until she gave the blanket up, but she struggled for the next few hours with its release. At one point, she said impatiently, *"Why is it taking so damned long?"* I said, *"Mom, take as long as you want. It's all up to you."*

Later she said, *"I've never seen anyone hold onto their silly blankets for so damned long!"* There was a woman named Bernadette who lived in town and had a handicapped child. I did not know her, but people who were with us said she was a saint with a big heart. She and my mom were friends, although I don't know how close they were. As Mom lay on the other side, dealing with the release of her blanket, Bernadette appeared to her. She stayed with mom on the other side until her last breath. Bernadette was the one who was finally able to take Mom's blanket. We listened as Bernadette coaxed her into feeling safe enough to give it up so she could move on. And then we heard Mom say, *"OK, Bernie. I am ready. Yes, you are right. Give it a tug for humanity; they don't have much."*

It's hard to believe that someone living could be on the other side of the veil with someone who is in the process of dying, but I heard it explained this way once. *"We as humans are but a piece of who we truly are as a whole spirit being. While we struggle to learn and grown on earth, our higher selves oversee our lives and step in every once in a while to make choices for us. If you call this being forth in times of need for strength and wisdom, he or she will assist you."* Believing in this, Bernie's higher self or spirit was there with mom to help her with her process. As we pass over and are received on the other side, I also believe that not only those loved ones who have already passed over are there to greet us, but also the spirit bodies or higher selves of those who are still alive. So when Mom would finally pass over, all of her children and her family would be there to greet her with open arms and open hearts. Even her sister, Jeannette, would be there. They would meet again and embrace each other with love.

Speak my name–
so that I might know you,
and take you–
into my soul.

Chapter 10

"Always"

In between the conversations Mom was having with the other side, she was reviewing her life. Her mom was with her. I don't remember exactly when Grammy came in to be with her, but Mom called her "Mummy". That is what I remember her calling her when I was a child. I heard her ask, *"Mummy, is he here?"* I'm sure she was asking about her dad. She talked about people from her childhood. On the third day, she would move on into her adulthood and review her relationships there, greeting those people.

On that second day when her speech was good, she handled her pain so well, she was funny. I never knew until that last week, just how funny Mom could be. This was the side of her I hadn't known. She had everyone belly-laughing as she lay there dying. It was outrageous! She teased cousin Bob about flirting with the pretty nurses, using phrases and words I cannot write in this book. I've toned her remarks down a bit. At one point during this long, emotional process, Lisa was crying and said, *"Gail, do you think it's taking so long because she keeps swearing so much that they won't take her into* heaven?" I said, *"No, Lisa. It doesn't matter. She can swear all she wants. They love her anyway."*

Mom loved cousin Kathy. She loved Kathy to tell her stories. She lived her life exactly like I did, seizing every moment, I think Mom lived vicariously through her and her stories. My high school girlfriend stopped by and Mom had her laughing uncontrollably. They would come in weeping, full of sadness, and then leave laughing with a smile on their faces. I had heard somewhere that the key to mastering the "self" was in being able to turn sadness and anger into love and joy. I had been taught to do it with the breath and meditation, though I still hadn't mastered it. Mom had mastered it with laughter as though it were no big deal.

I sat on her bed those last days, waiting. I wanted to wait and would have waited forever. She was my mom. She was the mom I had never allowed myself to experience. I loved her so much. She lay there making little cooing noises and sighing as I rubbed lotion on her hands, feet, and her beautiful bald head. She told me how good it felt and how good it smelled. Those tiny things were her heaven as she lay there. I loved sitting and sharing them with her. She had stopped eating on Wednesday, so she drank water and savored the ice chips. Something so simple as ice chips is so precious and so wondrous to the dying.

As she relived her life, I remembered those sad times that still made me sad, but as I saw her relive or review them from a higher place, they did not seem to bring sadness for her. They just "were." Those were such profound moments. And then as we sat there contemplating this overwhelming process called death, she would come out with, *"I've worn some of the ugliest damned shoes!"* as if she were reviewing every pair of shoes she had ever worn!

It is a strange thing to live through lack of sleep. In the beginning, you feel you can't do it, that you can't take another step or say another word because your brain cells are sleeping. You feel as though you can't blink your eyes one more time or they will slam shut and you won't have the strength to open them. At first you are whiney, but then you get over it. You just do it. All you feel is pure emotion. Every time Mom moaned, I was up from my seat in a flash. So were the others. We ran on emotion and caffeine. Caffeine does serve a purpose after all.

Somewhere in the middle of the third day, mom said, *"Oh, they're having a party for me! Look who just walked in! Oh!"* They were having a party in her honor on the other side! She was delighted, and she shared with us her vision of all the people who came to see her. One by one, she greeted friends and family as they arrived, both here in our world and there on the other side. To me, I would have been exhausted, but she wasn't. Her energy seemed to be revitalized with every new encounter. To all of those at the party as they arrived, she said, *"Oh, it's so nice to see you. I have every one of your pictures!"* Each one who came in, she called by name: *"Mr. Bigg, Wayne, Neil, Teresa and Rick,"* to which she said, *"Oh, Teresa and Rick, you made it! I didn't think you would. I'm so happy you did!"* They loved Mom and had adopted her as their Mom, though she had lived so far away. Because they lived out of state, by the time we found their phone number, it was too late for them to come to see her. At least they had made it to the party they were throwing for her.

Then she began to negotiate with the powers that be for more time. This was on the third day. "*Please, just give me a little more time. That's all I need. All right then, you can stop the water. I have to wait until 4 am?"* A lot of these one-sided conversations, we could only guess about. Some of them we understood; some we did not and couldn't even guess. Each time she moved to another level of the nine levels, she met with friends and loved ones who spoke with her. We sat on her bed holding her hands day in and day out. My brother did, also. Her grandchildren and niece were there with her, also, weeping as they walked in, and laughing as they walked out. So many people came to visit her. On the last two days, there were so many; we finally asked them to cut their visits short, not for her so much as for us. The only reason we thought to do this was because cousin Bob recommended it. We were so lost in all the company and the outpouring of love from everyone.

The days turned into nights and all three of us sisters slept wherever we were. We took turns on a bed next to Mom's since they were able to move her to another room. But the one who got to sleep in the bed for a few hours seemed to be up continually anyway. Every time she made a sound, we all bolted to be next to her. With lack of sleep and such high emotions, we started to weep more often. Then she would open her eyes wide and say something like, *"It's not going to happen today, ladies."* Then she would shut her eyes again. We would burst out into hysterical laughter. The thing I will remember most about her passing is the laughter we shared. That is how she healed us and brought us closer together.

In those last days, we didn't know up from down or right from wrong. Every paradigm we knew shifted or changed. We didn't know what we were feeling, or how to define the grief. To us, it was sadness and sorrow, happiness and joy, laughter, elation, a feeling of togetherness, caring, compassion and love. Love was what it was, anyway.

I had been struggling with working too hard in my life and carrying the burden of grief for my dying mother for the last eleven months. So I had not been fun to be around and had often been depressed. The day before I got on the plane, I told myself I needed to laugh more and have more fun. I needed to get out more, too. On this Sunday night my mom opened her eyes and said to me, *"Gail, don't let the stress of this world take you over. It'll eat you up."* How could she know what had been in my head and in my heart? We hadn't talked about these things. These were the words of wisdom from a dying mother. She knew.

That day, at one point, she opened her eyes wide as I was

holding her hand, and she said, *"I almost slipped, Gail! No, not yet!"* We saw her make peace with everyone in her life. Her harsh feeling toward men softened in those last days. She talked about Dad and other men she had dated who had left her angry during her life. Now she talked about them with love and compassion and even said things like, *"You know he did treat me very well at times."* She started to recognize the lessons she had learned as though she saw these situations through different eyes. She let her heart open up and experienced her review from a different perspective. It was awesome to watch.

On this day before she passed, she could not really speak much, but when she could, it was always with profound wisdom. *"I'm sorry you all have to go through this,"* not sorry for herself, but for those she loved. And later she would say, "*Do you know what it feels like to go through this?*" We huddled closer to her on the bed so we wouldn't miss the wisdom, and her simple response came: "*Nothing. It feels like nothing.*" That was another giddy moment for me. When my ego got out of control and I thought I was so smart that I knew more about death than anyone else in the room, I was surprised with her simple words that sounded so true.

I learned to stay out of my ego and just be with her with an open heart. That would create a space for love and "no fear." This is the space that the dying want to be in before passing. It is a safe, peaceful place where they are surrounded by love, therefore, not lonely. Mom's biggest fear was dying alone. She wasn't lonely with all the love around her. If there were any egos in that room at any given time, it was only mine. And I learned throughout the process when it needed to go "sit by the river in meditation" so to speak, so that my heart would be available for her.

That day, every time someone walked into the room, Mom

asked for Glenn. By evening, her beautiful blue eyes had clouded over and she could no longer see. Glenn and Mom had had a very rocky relationship. She was very hard on him because he was married to her baby girl and because he was a man. Sometimes he had to withstand a great deal of anger that was bottled up inside of her–anger that he didn't deserve. He let it roll off his back because he loved my sister and Mom. He was there when she needed him. Glenn was the one Lisa had called to lift her and carry her into the hospital. Now, as she looked for him, she said he was the only one she trusted to lift her, because she felt safe in his strong arms.

Sunday afternoon, Bob had been downstairs and came up to tell us that my father had been brought in to the emergency room. How ironic. How odd that on this day, he would have chosen to bring himself here? I walked down to see him and went toward him. He was sitting up in a chair next to his wife, Marie. I went to hug him and he said, *"Gail, don't. I'm in too much pain."* And then he burst into tears like a baby. Everyone thought it was for the pain in his back. (His bones were so brittle that he kept breaking them). I knew the tears were for my mother. I am sure on some level, he was grieving for her and would miss talking with her. He never did get to see her. When I got back upstairs, I told mom he was in the building. I said, *"Wouldn't it be something if you both passed over at the same time?"* She said, *"Gail, we already have."* I'm sure she knew what she meant and he was there with her on the other side with everyone else. That Sunday was very special, because we knew her time was short.

For each of those four days that I called California to speak with my son and friends, I told them that she would pass on that day that I called. I had been so sure. But she was still with us. On the fifth day, Monday, I called in the early morning to leave messages with everyone and I said, *"I don't know anything. I thought she would pass, but I don't know now. It could be a few more days for all I know."* I thought I knew everything once again. I thought I had it all figured out. I thought this passing would not be difficult. I thought it would be quick and that would be it. We would walk back into our lives easily. I thought I had mended my relationship with my mother and that I understood everything. I even shared those thoughts with friends before I left. I had made my peace with her and loved her. I understood why I chose her for my birth mother and what lessons she had taught me to make me strong and open my heart. I had it all figured out and wrapped up in a neat little box with a ribbon wrapped around it.

But it wasn't that simple. I had no idea I would experience these thoughts and emotions the last few days of her life and that my heart would expand and open up, and that my soul would be so exposed. I had no idea that during that last week, my journey had just begun.

When you prepare for the passing of a loved one, they are not the only ones whose lives flash before them; we also experience it. In those five days, everything in my life had passed before me with a clearer vision. I was looking at it from a new perspective called "love with more understanding." I can't explain it. Every circumstance, every situation, every relationship, every heart awakening experiencing in my life was viewed by me from a higher perspective. I had clarity on what was important and the importance of friends and family, a mother, a father, and also the innocence of the children. I was expanded, all because of the love of my mother. Her greatest gift to me was that precious five-day span.

I saw a different person. I saw more than just the mother she was to me. I saw who she was to other people, a dear friend, a surrogate mother, a grandmother, a nurturer, a sweet loving mother to my sister. I had never stopped long enough to see these things before. Someone very dear to my heart, my spiritual advisor, asked me how I was doing through all of this. I told him that everything I had known to be true about my relationship with my mother was different from what I was experiencing. I was so confused. Had I been wrong all those years? This wasn't the mother I knew. I was feeling guilt for how I had seen her and therefore, how I had reacted and interacted with her in my mother/daughter relationship.

My spiritual advisor said to me, *"When we come into this world as humans, we come in with our egos, a mask, so to speak. This mask, neither good nor bad, is who we are. We wear one for our daughters and one for our sons, our husbands and wives, our friends. It is who we are and how we deal with and react to each situation. It is our ego. When the spirit decides it is ready for rebirth and the body is ready to die, the ego says", **"I'm out of here!!!"** "And the mask fades. Isn't it wonderful that you got to experience the expanded being she was after the mask had faded? What a wonderful thing for you!"*

That gave me clarity. I was no longer confused. I thought I had been mistaken with my view of our relationship–but this was a confirmation that I had done the best I could at all those times I was now questioning. When I chose to move to the west coast, I knew I had to do that to survive.

She was in and out of consciousness that day, her breathing rattled. She was no longer taking fluid or even savoring the ice chips she loved so much. We mostly sat in silence around her bed or talked softly with each other. We were waiting. At one point, she called her children to her bed and said, *"I'm going out the same way I came in . . . with a tear in my eye for each of you,"* and she went on to tell us she loved us. She said to remember the song "Always" because she used to sing it to us when we were little. And she sat there with Kathy, singing every word:

"Everything went wrong
and the whole day long,
I'd feel so blue.

For the longest while,
I'd forget to smile,
Then I met you.

Now that my blue days have ended,
Now that I've found you at last,
I'll be loving you always,
With a love that's true, always.

When the things you plan
Need a helping hand,
I will understand, always.

Always—

Days may not be fair, always.
That's when I'll be there, always.
Not for just an hour–
Not for just a day–
Not for just a year–
But always."

I have never felt such love or grieved so much for loss in this special memory that I would forever treasure. On the day she finished painting the ceiling and the walls, she said, *"Oh, look! It's not blue, but a lilac. How pretty!"* I asked, *"Mom, who painted it with you?"* She said, *"Why Red, of course."* She stopped painting that day and was satisfied with that color that she loved. We heard her whisper, *"We're holding up a lot of people here. I'm ready. I want to go."*

So we sat there and waited and squeezed her hand. I rubbed her feet and her head with lotion. She was so funny. The whole time she was in the hospital, she wanted her feet out of the sheets. She did not want them covered up at all and everyone knew it. If a new nurse came on staff and didn't know her, we would let her know immediately. It is also one of my quirks that I don't like the weight of the sheets on my toes and can't sleep if I feel them. This was something I had never known about Mom.

We sat through the night in that state of surreal grace where we didn't know what time it was or if it were moving at all. We didn't even know who we were anymore. We just "were." She had been in the sleep state for a few hours when we heard her breath become very slow. Lisa started to cry and then we all started crying loudly. She opened her eyes and said, *"Now, ladies, don't you think we're a little overtired here?"* We burst into laughter. Only Mom could do this on her deathbed.

"It is time to go to sleep
and open your eyes on the other side.

Prepare yourself for slumber, and
dream the dreams of God.

As you lie in your bed, look upward,
and show yourself
for both worlds to see.

Awaken to a new day, with new joys–
new life–
and new love.

It is all waiting for you–
through the new doorway–
the doorway to the kingdom
of your heart and mine."

Chapter 11

The Birth

Though we took turns sleeping that night, most of us were up walking around the room. She slept more deeply that night than all the others. And night continued, turning into another day, and in between the sleeping and the waking, she whispered, *"I am going up the stairs. Oh, what a beautiful prism of light! Look, it's getting larger. How beautiful!"* And then there was quiet for a while. And then we heard in the distance, *"I love you, Mother, Queen of the Angels. I love you, Jesus."* Those were the last words she spoke. She never awoke consciously after that. It was as if she were waiting in some sacred space until her soul left her body, ready to be received by God on the other side.

It happened about 1:25 p.m. that day. It was the most peaceful passing I have ever experienced. There was no fear, no doubt, and no lack of confidence or trust. She knew when it was time and she knew she controlled her passage. When she was finished, she was finished. And she took her last breath as the immediate family sat with her.

She did not struggle for that last breath. She went easily and gently, her breath stopping as smoothly as it flowed. There was no fear because it seemed she chose when she would take that last breath. As it happened, we began crying. Lisa wailed. Mom had stopped breathing for almost five minutes at that point. As Lisa got louder, Mom opened her eyes, looked directly at Lisa, as if to say, *"That's enough! Get a grip on yourself,"* then she closed her eyes slowly and let the final breath out as she left her body for the final time. That broke the grief for that moment. I knew from that point on that she would be with me when I needed her. She proved that to me in that moment.

We sat with her for three hours after she passed and we still held her hands and touched her as though she were still alive. I felt this was important. I had heard that even though we think the soul has left when the body dies, sometimes they are still either in the room or still attached to the body somehow. I also didn't want to leave her. We sat at her side making all the arrangements for her service as if she were making them with us. I felt her hands grow colder and watched as the blood left her fingers, hands and feet. It was strange sitting with the dead and the dead being someone you loved. It wasn't frightening. It was a sweet time that I will always remember and cherish. As I looked back over the last few days, I realized that as she lay there in the final stages of her death, she was never cold, nor hungry nor thirsty. She was well taken care of, I am sure, by God and his legions of angels. They were there with her caring for her every need. And she needed nothing from us but our open hearts, and that is what we gave her.

I believe that when a human being dies, all they want is reassurance and support. They want you to sit with them so they are not alone and they want you to stay out of your sorrow and fear. As we sat in our hearts and not our egos with Mom, we helped her move peacefully toward her soul's purpose in that moment. Just by being there for her, we helped her pass over easily and lovingly. And my beliefs calmed me in knowing that the soul or the spirit drops the body, a borrowed body of sorts. This shell or body that protects the soul falls away so we can be reborn into the world we truly came from, the kingdom of god. This earth is a school to most and a playground to some, but a "plane of demonstration" where we choose to play poorly, play well, or not play at all.

Our immediate emotion was deep grief but after a while, there was relief and peace. It came from knowing that after all the communications she had shared with us, we knew she had gone to a place where she was loved so deeply. She had been received by God, as all of us will be. Lisa said, *"I feel guilty, Gail. I feel relieved like I am at peace with this."* I said, *"Lisa, you have grieved for eleven long and hard months. It's ok that you feel this way. This is how Mom wants you to feel."* Then, I felt a sadness. I realized I was no longer a mother's child. That hit me very hard. It was a deep emptiness that I thought might be there always.

We went about the day preparing for the service. Mom had been angry with the Catholic Church for thirty-seven years since they had turned their back on her when she told them she was leaving her physically abusive, alcoholic husband. She stated in her will that she didn't want to be "waked" or have a mass. So we went to the funeral parlor our family had always gone to and explained the situation. They were very helpful in giving us alternative options. My brother and sisters didn't want a wake, but all of those people in town that came to the hospital needed some way or somewhere to say good-bye to her. We debated back and forth about what it would be called and finally decided to call it a "*time to pay last respects.*" A service would follow immediately after this designated time. She eventually wanted to be cremated and her ashes strewn over the sea. But for these days of ceremony, her body was in a closed casket so that she would physically be there at her own service. How odd that we knew she was no longer in the body, but we feel the body should be present. Maybe this was out of respect that the body had taken such great care of the soul?

On top of the casket, we placed a beautiful picture of her when she was twenty years younger surrounded by white roses and gardenias, her favorite flowers. Mom would never allow anyone to take a picture so we had very few to choose from. This was how I always remembered her anyway. We placed her crystal votive candleholder next to the picture and one of the pieces from her clown collection. It was a raggedy clown with a big grin on his face and his arms raised on either side of his head, sticking his tongue out. This was how mom would want to be remembered. This was her. How appropriate that they would file in weeping and then break into laughter when they came to the coffin. She wanted to remind people to remember her with a smile or a joke.

There were a few hundred people who came. I had no idea she was so well loved in this small town I grew up in. Everyone came, even the nurses from ICU and her chemo and radiation nurses. I learned something new about her once again and was proud. My brother and sisters all did so well. All Mom's grandchildren and her niece had a difficult time as the eulogy was delivered. Bob spoke, and then Kathy, then I spoke. It was something I just knew I wanted to do. I sat down the morning after her death and asked Mom to be with me and assist me in writing exactly how she wanted to be remembered. This is what we wrote and what I spoke:

"I believe that when we pass over, it is a rebirth of our spirit. I feel strongly about this, though I have never experienced it. We can be told something extraordinary, but until we experience it first-hand, we do not know it to be true.

We as humans are like baby spirits. Our human bodies protect us like a shell, like the shell of a baby bird. As we live our lives, we grow and learn, until we reach a point in our existence where we have learned our life's lessons and have served our purpose and are ready to be born. Our shells crack at death and as we pass over to the other side, we are born into the spirit bodies that we truly are. For this is what we have always been.

And a large party is thrown for us by our loved ones. Our guides, our angels, our watchers, the beloved mother Mary, our beloved Sananda, or Jesus–all who have passed. And everyone comes.

I had the honor and the privilege to be with my Mom as she went through the stages of her rebirth. We were so blessed to be with her and to hear her speak in those last few days about what she was experiencing.

The miracle was that the cancer in her brain was affecting her speech so that she could not form words or finish sentences toward the end. And miraculously, she was able to have two days where she shared pearls of wisdom and her humor with us.

She took us on her journey with her. She painted the walls and the ceiling with her friends and her dog, Red. She kept changing the colors until she reached a lilac hue. Then she said, "What a beautiful color!" Lilac or lavender is the color of God, the holiest of colors.

She said she needed to make it to the ninth level before her passage and we listened to her as she journeyed there. Each time she climbed to a new level, she met with friends and loved ones who reminisced with her.

Her mother was there. She called her "Mummy."

She asked for three more days that last week to complete her journey and she was granted that wish.

She told us, "I'm going out the exact same way I came in with each of you, with a tear in my eye."

When she said she was ready and wanted to go toward the end. We sat and cried our hearts out for our loss. Yet she made it very clear that she did not want that.

Her sense of humor was incredible. We were sitting on her bed one of the last nights, crying uncontrollably and she opened her eyes and said very strongly, "Now ladies, don't you think we're just overtired here?"

At one point as she was reviewing her life, she said, "I've worn some of the ugliest damned shoes!"

As she was going through the chemo and radiation, she told those who were fortunate enough to spend time with her, "Don't think you are going to forget about me, because when you look up in the corner of the room and see a speck of dust, that's me; so don't brush me down." During the entire time, which was so hard for everyone else to watch, she had jokes for the doctors, the nurses and anyone else she encountered.

Even as she lay dying, she, "I'm sorry you have to go through this . . . I feel so bad for all of you."

My mother collected clowns throughout her life. They were her prized possession. I never understood the meaning of those clowns until her passing. Her sense of humor got her through her life. She told me two days before, "Gail, you need to laugh more. Don't let the stress of this world take you over."

I am honored to be her daughter. She was a queen who had mastered her life and given so much from the heart. Her purpose was to give to her four children and those who knew her, the gifts of humor, dignity, integrity, truth, honor, deep compassion, love and beauty. She didn't measure her life by material things. She found accomplishment, acceptance and peace in the simple life she had.

On the last night, she spoke these words:

"Oh, look! A beautiful prism of light!
"I love you, Mother, Queen of the Angels.
"I love you, Jesus."

My mom does not want any of us to remember her through tears, or with a broken heart. She wants us to laugh and tell jokes and remember her with a smile. We also have to remember, it is a glorious day of celebration, for she has been reborn into her place in heaven, sitting on her throne next to God, after her long journey here on earth."

Chapter 12

Send In the Clown

I was amazed at the outpouring of love and support from the people in this town and in the community. I had been gone for twenty-one years, not really seeing or visiting anyone when ever I had come home, I never stayed long enough. But old friends from high school came to support each one of us now. Past boyfriends' mothers came, and the mother of a sweet friend that had been killed in a car accident after high school. I was so moved by all the love and compassion. My sister's husband's family came in droves. It was a large family. And before and after the services, I watched my sister in her life with her friends and family. Many stopped by her home with flowers and meals and cards. They asked if they could do anything to help and made it clear that they would be there if she or anyone of us needed them. They asked if they could carpool her boys for her and her husband.

I wept for myself, for the fact that I had never given that kind of support to anyone. I felt I had no deep bonds. I was just beginning to learn how to be a supportive and loving friend who was there always. I had never experienced friendship like this. Lisa hadn't been afraid to open her heart and her arms to other people. She had supported them with love, compassion and tenacity, and she was now receiving the same in return.

During this experience of Mom's illness and death I came to know my long lost relatives, Bob, Kathy, Roy and his family.

I also learned to love my brother as an adult and his daughter, my niece. My brother and I were so close growing up, especially in our teen years. It felt so warm to be with him again. A few friends I had known since high school were there for me also, though I hadn't spoken much to them over the years. They were doing whatever it took, whatever I needed them to do. I was given a car for my use for the entire time I was there, I was taken to dinner one night, and they came to the hospital every day and ran errands for us. I had learned this week the true meaning of friendship. Friendship wasn't, "*Let's do lunch*," as they sometimes say in my part of the country, or saying hello via e-mail. It was human contact and support. It was being empathetic and being there for the duration.

I walked away from this a new person; I was humbled. Nothing seemed to fit anymore: my life, my name–all of those things I had identified myself with before. It would take months for me to find out where I now fit. And as the services drew to a close, my learning was still taking place. My siblings and I went through Mom's belongings. I wanted to help as much as I could before I had to go back home. I could at least be the emotional support that everyone needed and clean out as much as I could for my sister. I knew how hard it would be for her to go through mom's clothing especially.

As we went through the process of sorting out the material things of her life, that was a process for me, also. She didn't have much at all. She had a few plates and cups and bowls. She had the necessities like pots and pans. Her only other possessions were the clowns she collected and lots of cards from her children, grandchildren and friends. I couldn't believe it. Some of them went back twenty years. I read through them and realized that I had held my son back from having a close relationship with his grandma because of how I had felt about her. Now I was very sad about that. Living far away had been no excuse. My niece, Hannah, who lived eight hours away, had loved her grandma so much that she had visited often. I read the sweetness and the love in all the cards to Mom.

Mom treasured every event, every accomplishment her grandchildren achieved. I was so sad for my losses. They were unrecoverable. Now I had to live with myself and forgive myself. I went through her clothing with my sister Carol and helped her pack them up so she could take them with her. I took Mom's pajamas because when I had visited her I always seemed to forget my own. I'd sleep in hers and they'd keep me warm. I have worn them almost every night for months, just because they were a part of her.

Taking Mom's clothing from her closets was hardest on Lisa. That's why I did it so quickly. She didn't want any part of it. Mom had very little in the closet but you would never know it. At least I never knew it, and I was her daughter. Although the financial woes were often heavy and overwhelming to her, she held her head high. She was rich within herself.

Mom and I had talked briefly about her dying. I told her that when she was ready and wanted to talk, I would be there. I asked her once if she was afraid to die and she said, *"No, I'm not afraid at all."* I know she had been thinking about it and preparing for it because we found this poem tucked away near her kitchen table. It was close to her day-to-day things, like her crossword puzzles, which she kept close by. She probably read it often:

"Do not stand on my grave and weep;
I am not there; I do not sleep.
I am a thousand winds that blow.
I am the diamonds that glint the snow.
I am the sunlight in a ripened grain.
I am a gentle autumn's rain.
When you awaken in the morning's hush,

I am the soft, uplifting rush,
of quiet birds in circled flight.
I am the soft stars that shine at night.
Do not stand at my grave and cry.
I am not there.
I did not die.

—Author Unknown

For the remainder of the days that I was there, I slept in my mom's bed and spent time with my sisters and brother. It was a time of mixed emotions. We were at peace and even laughed a little in the days that followed–sometimes feeling guilty when we were happy . . . but only for a moment. We always reminded each other of what Mom would say about that. If we forgot to remind each other, she would do something to remind us. Lisa was at mom's trailer the very night she passed over and opened the refrigerator door. A magnet flew off the door that read, *"You have the face only a mother could love."* It was so appropriate, because Mom always teased Lisa about wearing her feelings on her sleeve, or her face. If she was unhappy, there was no hiding it with Lisa.

We were still going to bed past 1:00 a.m. because there were so many things to take care of, yet I still awoke around 8:00 a.m. My sister Carol was asleep on the pullout couch in the parlor. I had just opened my eyes and was trying to get in touch with how I was feeling at that moment. All of a sudden, I heard one of Mom's wind-up clowns go off. It played its tune for probably two minutes. It couldn't have been bumped. It played as though it had been wound up. And then the phone rang as soon as it stopped. It was a wrong number. I found out later that Lisa's mother-in-law, who had helped care for Mom and had been a wonderful friend to her, was thinking about Mom that morning a little after eight o'clock. She said, *"Your mother was on my mind. I couldn't stop thinking about her and I went to dial my daughter, but dialed your mom's number instead! I'm sorry I woke you!"* I said, *"Margaret, it's okay. It was Mom playing a joke on us. She's just reminding us she's still with us."*

A FEATHER

A feather–

floating

gently,

lazily,

downward –

from heaven

dropping

into

my

lap –

reminding me:

"I am here
if you should need me.
Just look upward
with your heart."

As the end of the week came, we all had to go back to our lives and our jobs. We had been away for a while. This was difficult. We had shared this special space with each other and shared a lot of special love. Even when we met up again for the reunion we promised each other–it would never be like this. This was a time of healing and sharing and mending and loving deeply—more deeply than any of us had probably ever allowed.

As Bob held us and hugged us, he thanked us for allowing him to share this experience. with him and with our family for that week. That was how we felt. It was an honor to have shared this time with my mother and with him, Kathy, Roy, his wife Karen and his daughter Christina. Mom was the one who had brought us all back together. She was sly! I could feel her over my shoulder laughing with glee as we said our good-bye's.

It was hardest for my sister Lisa. As Glenn drove us to the airport, we were very somber. I didn't want to leave her and she didn't want to leave me. I think we thought that if we parted, we wouldn't be strong enough to deal with this emotionally. I was frightened to go back to my life and leave the strength, the love and the warmth of my family behind with my sister. We held each other and cried until it was time to go. It was again one of the most difficult things I have had to do.

Chapter 13

The Gift

When I got to California, my son was so sweet and supportive, my ex-husband and his new wife were very supportive, and my friends had done incredible things for me and continued to help me when I returned. I could feel their friendship now differently than before. It was deeper. Maybe it was just that my heart was now open so I could feel more of their love. My heart had expanded. I thought for a moment that I wanted to make sure it didn't close again.

The cards I received were so heart-felt. Every word written touched me so. I was moved by the love and human compassion surrounding me.

> *"Dear Gail, please accept my condolences on the death of your mother. I would be happy to share with you my feelings on when I lost both my parents. The feelings I experience, I believe, are common to the grieving process, and it always was helpful to me to be able to share the burden with a friend, as I worked back toward a more normal place in my life. Please don't hesitate to ask for help. I will gladly be there for you at this most difficult time."*

Another wrote:

> *"May the Lord provide all the strength you will need*

on this journey. My thoughts, prayers and love will be with you."

This was from a woman who had lost her son to suicide.

Another:

". . . just know my heart and spirit surrounds yours in the healing process of such a loss. . ."

Another:

"When one thinks he or she knows death,
they are deceived . . .
when one experiences death,
this is knowing and love is perceived.
When one journeys this process full circle,
wisdom is gained.
This, my dear Gail, is the relationship with The One."

Another:

"I have heard about your mom's passing–I keep getting the feeling and image that all our moms are now these beautiful bridges for us–their daughters–and that always feels good to me. I share this with you, hoping you will find comfort when the missing comes up. We are all one, even in the missing, and especially in the loving. I love you, sweet one."

Another:

"May you walk in peace and silence, and you will hear your soul speak."

Another:

"You have my deepest sympathy. I know how dear my own mother is to me and I sympathize with your loss."

Another:

"I was very sorry to hear about your mother. I am sure she was a remarkable woman, just as you are."

Another:

"I recently heard someone say that grieving is the tax we pay for loving someone . . . that the mother/ daughter relationship is one of the most complicated we will ever experience, and that bond, the strongest, next to that of our children–makes this time of your life all the more poignant.

"I know it may sound so strange that the rest of the world is going by as if nothing has changed, when for you, your whole world has been forever altered . . . You are in my heart and thoughts."

And finally:

"Dear Gail,

I know it is hard to understand that those who have given life, now themselves lay lifeless . . . a true passing of one generation to the next, I suppose. What we can understand and do know, is that those we have loved and lost, will live on through us in our memories, our actions, our characteristics, our look and even a simple saying.

Have you ever said to yourself, 'Mom used to say that all the time,' or 'I sound like my mother!' My mom used to say and still does, "You kids are driving me up one wall and down the other!' Now I say it to my husband! A piece of my mom–a part of me.

OK. This might be taking it a little too far, but it made you smile, didn't it? So even during the worst of times, we can muster up a smile. As time passes, the smiles come more frequently and seem to stay a little longer each time if we let them. Allow time for sorrow, but also, allow time for happiness.

We always forget that dying is a part of life, and we must remember that the two come hand in hand. Death is a life experience with a reward of pain-free, peaceful bliss. Gail, to your mother, I wish 'Sweet Dreams!'

Each word written to me came from someone's heart. They were gifts that I would hold close forever. I had finally learned to release, accept and allow love to touch me deeply. I could feel it now. I could feel the love of my mother, the love of my son, my friends, my lover; I could feel their hearts opening to my pain, and at last I opened my heart to them.

A few weeks after I got back, I received a portion of Mom's ashes. Her request was that we sprinkle her over the Cape Cod Canal. Because the ashes weren't ready before I had to leave, my sister and her family had strewn them over the water and mailed me a small urn. On this particular Friday, I drove down the coast to the quaint town of Encinitas where my beloved cliffs were, with Swami's Beach below. This was my special place for Mom and me. I visited her there often. It's funny that the day was cold and drizzly and overcast like a New England day. It was so appropriate. I found a little Italian café and had a lunch of shrimp stuffed with lobster. You could hardly see or taste the lobster, but it was my memorial meal to Mom and and of course it should include lobster. After I finished eating, I sat and wrote the end of the first draft of this book and was saddened because I knew it was coming to an end.

I thought this last ritual of scattering her ashes into the wind and sea would be easy until the release itself, and then that it would be hard to let her go. It was the opposite. A soon as I got into my car, I started to weep. I wept all day, though it was hours before I would release her. I wasn't quite ready. I sat on the beach and watched some Tibetan monks in their bright orange robes walking along the rocks, picking up the smooth stones. I knew I was in good hands. If they were here with their open hearts filled with God, then this was the place. As I walked into the water and stood there letting the waves wash over me, I said a prayer and said good-bye to her. I finally released her spirit into the wind and into the waves, to freedom from this life and its struggle. Now she was part of the world. "I am a thousand winds that blow." As soon as I released all of her, I felt a bliss fill my being. I felt her in my heart and in my lungs as I breathed in the air. I felt as though she were inside of me. I was closer to her now than I had ever felt, as though we were one and the same.

I feel closer to Mom more now than ever before, and I have spoken to many women recently who have lost their mothers and feel the same. They, too, feel their mothers inside of them. It is strange . . . I feel less longing for a mother now than I did all of my life.

TO MOTHER

You were always there for me–for us.
We closed our eyes and walked blindly by
with our hands out, palms to the air in front of us–
looking for you,
always calling your name–
But you were right in front of us–
waiting for us to touch you.

Our masks were pulled down too tightly,
and too low, over our eyes,
hiding our souls and shielding our hearts.
All we had to do was
reach out and touch–
your hand–your heart.

So now,
now that you have passed,
we have let our masks down,
and let you in.
So you ride with us–
on the tides of our hearts–
inside of us.

I thank you, Mom, for your love and your strength and the gift you gave me of allowing me to be your daughter.

I LOVE YOU!

THE BUTTERFLY

The butterfly–
flitting so beautifully–
so softly–
so gently.

Fluttery.
Dancing on the air.
Each moment is a breath–
so rhythmic.

Outstretched wings–
as if they were
angels of the sky.

Reborn from their cocoon,
as we are–
as our souls fly free
from our bodies.

Conclusion

After my mother passed over, I wasn't sure how I could possibly walk back into my life and carry on. I no longer fit inside it, and was forever changed. The strength that I had gathered from my family was a new experience for me and I was only able to gain that strength by dropping my ego—my protective shield of armor that I wore in this life—and to open my heart and let everyone in. This was a frightening thing for me, because I only knew love to mean pain.

After Mom's death, I realized the pain was only part of the riches, the knowledge, the joy, the wisdom, the passion—the whole experience. If I had closed myself off so as not to get hurt, I would have missed out on the entire experience of being with Mom and seeing the incredible woman I had not seen before. I only hope that I have her strength, her courage, her humor and her grace when it is my time.

Mom was a simple woman who I never understood when she was alive. I didn't understand why she didn't want more from life, but I soon learned she was quite content with herself and what she had created. She found happiness in simplicity and importance in family and friends.

When I returned home to California, I looked at the world through a new pair of eyes and with a new heart that lay open like an open wound. Each new encounter with people felt like someone pouring salt in that wound. It was very painful, but I eventually got used to this and it healed. My life is full and enriched right now. I have learned a lot about love and compassion.

If I have any advice, it would be to love deeply and to love hard. Remember that we come into this life with a mask that protects us. If we remember this, we will be able to drop that mask and truly love our mother, father, and siblings. For soon, they will leave us behind as they continue their journeys home. Do not have any regrets in this lifetime and please, forgive them and forgive yourself. You are doing the best you can in every moment!

About the Author

Gail Michael, formerly Gail Elizabeth Henricks was born in Taunton Massachusetts in 1954. She attended high school and college in Taunton and Fall River, Mass., and then moved to southern California when she was 25 years old. She then attended the University of California, Los Angeles while living in the San Gabriel Valley.

Gail's life has led her on an unusual quest, seeking truth, wisdom, and the understanding of forgiveness, love, and compassion. As her consciousness has unfolded with her studies, she has had a great love affair with her pen, telling tales of her journeys inside her heart and how all that she has learned has affected the way she views life. Her poetry has been published in many publications, including *The American Poetry Annual* by The Amherst Society, and *Celebrations of the Heart* by The Poetry Center.

Gail has worked in procurement for over twenty-five years. She currently resides in Orange County with her teenage son, and works as a purchasing manager for a medical device manufacturer.For more information about Gail, you may view her website at **www.gail-michael.com**

9 26575 76119 4